I0644012

RESTORED POWER

Becoming a Praying Church One Tweak at a Time

Jonathan Graf

PRAYERSHOP PUBLISHING

Terre Haute, IN

PrayerShop Publishing is the publishing arm of Harvest Prayer Ministries and the Church Prayer Leaders Network. Harvest Prayer Ministries exists to transform lives through teaching prayer. Its online prayer store, www.prayershop.org, has more than 300 prayer resources available for purchase.

ISBN: 978-1-935012-66-5

1 2 3 4 5 | 2020 2019 2018 2017 2016

TABLE OF CONTENTS

PREFACE

RESTORING THE POWER OF GOD IN YOUR MIDST

FOR THE PAST TWENTY YEARS, I have been on a ministry journey that has had me focus primarily on helping churches become houses of prayer for all nations. "House of Prayer" was the name Jesus gave His Father's house (Isaiah 56:7; Matthew 21:13).

Over those years, I have seen churches take great strides in becoming praying churches. I have watched what has worked. Seen what has not. Observed both pitfalls and successes.

I have learned that growing a praying church is not easy! But it does not have to be daunting. I have learned that churches that persevere will get there.

Restored Power: Becoming a Praying Church One Tweak at a Time is a practical book about what I have learned over my many years of working with churches. I believe it will minister to you and your leaders as you seek to make prayer more central, more foundational to your ministry.

Restored Power is actually a sequel to *Forgotten Power: A Simple Theology for a Praying Church* by David Butts. If you picked up this book before seeing that one, I encourage you to get it as well. It presents in a clear way the theology of prayer. It will help your leaders get the "why" of prayer in your church. *Restored Power* will help with the "how."

As you read this book, I encourage you to pray and think. Ask the Holy Spirit to speak to you about what He wants to do in your midst. Ask Him to show you the way to see His power restored in your church.

– Jonathan Graf

INTRODUCTION

..‖ IT'S WORTH THE FIGHT ‖..

I WAS RECENTLY SPEAKING to a group of pastors at a denominational gathering on the state level. Their bishop had me come to teach about growing a praying church. It was a captive audience. (I suspect some received credit in some way for being there.)

I was very well received. I could see that most were buying into what I was saying. They believed that prayer was important, and many believed that it was the most important thing that could bring change to their churches. Many left fired up to try again to grow prayer.

But I left there wondering if real change would take place in their churches. They would make a valiant attempt to get prayer front and center to their ministry. But when they came up against indifference, or worse, opposition, especially from elders or deacons, would they have the heart and passion to fight for prayer?

Or when they came against the doers, who felt like people just needed to do more? "Prayer? We certainly pray. We need to do more than pray." Would they be able to convince, "No, we need more prayer"?'

Growing prayer is probably the most difficult thing to do in any church. Why? Bill Johnson, in *When Heaven Invades Earth*, hit the nail on the head: "The enemy's greatest efforts at deceiving the Church are centered on the purpose and effect of prayer." There is no other aspect of church life and function that the enemy wants to see less of than prayer. He will raise up opposition to it in every way possible.

And so we give up.

Restored Power is geared to help you not to give up and to provide manageable ways to tweak prayer, stimulate prayer, and motivate prayer in your church.

While I am all for doing whatever God tells you to do in growing prayer in your church, *Restored Power* will not tell you to shut down all ministries for six months and do nothing but pray. I won't even tell you that to be a praying church you have to have a midweek corporate prayer meeting. (Shh. Don't let my prayer leader friends know about that one!)

I believe that any church—no matter the size, theological stream, or governing polity—can become a prayer-based church. And I believe that it can happen over time, with some simple tweaking of attitudes and existing practices. But it will take some effort, and there will definitely be opposition. Lots of it. But it is worth it. No question.

As you begin raising the bar on prayer, you will see an atmospheric change and you will begin to see transformational change in the hearts and lives of people.

.: A CHURCH THAT LOST ITS WAY :.

A number of years ago, our ministry was called to help a local church through a transition to a new pastor. Could our speakers fill their pulpit over the summer? Our founder, Dave Butts, was asked to meet with the church elder board to help give them some direction.

I spoke there several Sundays, but two stood out: Father's Day and Fourth of July weekend. Both made me realize that something was drastically wrong.

On Father's Day, more time was spent focusing on dads than on Jesus. Even the worship was geared that way. I had to literally suppress laughter when an all-women choir (made up of about eight to ten ladies all over sixty-five) sang the song "Butterfly Kisses," which is supposed to be sung by a father to his daughter.

On the July 4th weekend, we did not sing a single worship song but rather had a morning of patriotism, singing "The Star Spangled Banner," "America the Beautiful," "My County 'Tis of Thee," and pledging allegiance to the flag. When I got up to preach, I wasn't sure if I should talk about George Washington or Jesus.

This was clearly a church that had lost it way. It did not know what it was to be about. It had become just a social club for the thirty-forty people who still attended there (most, their whole lives).

Having spent his life in the community, Dave had seen this once vibrant church diminish in ministry over the past few decades. The last decade had seen multiple pastors stay for two years or so and depart. They were stuck in the rut of tradition with no expectation of needing change.

When he met with the board, Dave said that one of three things needed to happen:

1. They could shut their doors now and sell off the church, donating the money to another ministry.
2. They could continue as they had been for as long as they could afford to keep the doors open. They would be making the decision just to minister to the people who were currently there, until they were gone.
3. Or they could determine that they needed to change drastically. It would be hard on people who were used to the way things had been, and it would take significant prayer, but they could be a viable ministry again.

They needed to pray about it and see what God wanted, then select that option.

They eventually chose option three (what could they do, but that?). They started praying together a little more as leaders. They eventually called Chris, a guy no longer pastoring a church who was working as a landscaper in the area. When Chris came, the first thing he did was take his leaders through Dave Butts's book, *The Devil Goes to Church,* which is a study on simple spiritual warfare that comes against what the enemy tries to do in a church. Most older churches that are in decline usually have sin issues in their midst that need to be dealt with, and this church was no exception.

Then Chris started shoring up the existing midweek prayer time, which had become entirely needs-based praying. He focused more on the move of God in the church and growth issues. And God started moving. Today, this congregation of thirty to forty aging saints is a vibrant congregation of 150 plus, with members across all age groups.

Prayer can do that for your church, too. Through prayer, God will restore His power in your midst. It is worth the effort and the fight.

CHAPTER 1

..‖ THE IMPORTANCE OF PRAYER IN ACTS ‖..

IMAGINE THE SITUATION. Jerusalem is absolutely abuzz. All of a sudden on one day, more than 3,000 people started following a new way—following Jesus Christ, a person that had been killed, but who, rumor had it, came alive again.

His followers—mostly common folk—were clearly shaking up the city. Those 3,000 followers of Christ probably represented 10 percent or so of the city's population! Every day, they came to the Temple to teach. Every day brought more individuals who believed the message—around 5,000 people by Acts 4:4.

The religious leaders were absolutely incensed at this. *We must do something to stop the spread of this cult,* they thought. Then there came a very visible display of power in front of everyone at the Temple. A man who was crippled from birth was healed by Peter and John. That was the last straw for the religious leaders.

So later that day, while Peter and John were teaching to a crowd, they sent temple police to arrest them. The police dragged Peter and John off in front of the people, then had them beaten and thrown into prison. Because it was late in the day, the leaders could not pull a tribunal together, so they let them sit in jail overnight.

The next morning they brought Peter and John in front of the high priest and synagogue leaders. Peter and John were threatened with their lives and commanded never to speak of this Jesus again. But because of the people, the leaders let them go.

Peter and John headed back to their group of fellow believers.

They needed to pray about this threat. But what should they pray?

That is the first story in Acts where we see a specific use of prayer in the early church. They were facing the first significant threat to the spread of the gospel.

Think about that for a moment. If that had happened to us, Western church leaders, what would we have prayed in that situation? I suspect that many of you—and our church—would pray this way: "Get me out of this." Or "Intervene Lord, remove these evil men from office." Or perhaps, "Lord, change their hearts." My mind would immediately go to praying a "fix-it" prayer, a "change this situation" prayer.

But what did these guys pray? Acts 4:23-30 records their prayer:

> On their release, Peter and John went back to their own people and reported all that the chief priests and the elders had said to them. When they heard this, they raised their voices together in prayer to God. "Sovereign Lord," they said, "you made the heavens and the earth and the sea, and everything in them. You spoke by the Holy Spirit through the mouth of your servant, our father David:
>
> "'Why do the nations rage
> and the peoples plot in vain?
> The kings of the earth rise up
> and the rulers band together
> against the Lord
> and against his anointed one.'
>
> Indeed Herod and Pontius Pilate met together with the Gentiles and the people of Israel in this city to conspire against your holy servant Jesus, whom you anointed. They did what your power and will had decided beforehand should happen. Now, Lord, consider their threats and enable your servants to speak your word with great boldness. Stretch out your hand to heal and perform signs and wonders through the name of your holy servant Jesus."
>
> After they prayed, the place where they were meeting was shaken. And they were all filled with the Holy Spirit and spoke the word of God boldly.

Instead of focusing prayer on changing the situation, they chose the kingdom-expansion approach. They prayed a different way than the modern church would have prayed.

What did the early church pray about? As I look at the role of prayer in Acts and its practice in the Church, I see not only that they recognized the importance of prayer and emphasized it far more than we do, but they also focused their prayer on different things than the things on which Western churches typically focus prayer. I truly believe if we could get the focus of our prayers right, the emphasis and importance would naturally follow.

.: KINGDOM OVER COMFORT :.

In this passage from Acts, we clearly see a situation where it would have been easy to ask for protection, escape, and/or change in the situation. But these early followers didn't even hint at those outcomes. "Now, Lord," they prayed, "consider their threats and enable your servants to speak your word with great boldness. Stretch out your hand to heal and perform signs and wonders through the name of your holy servant Jesus" (4:29-30).

They ask for more of the very thing that got them into trouble—a visible miracle. "Give us the enablement we need to proclaim your Word," they asked. "And let signs and wonders follow!" There was no thought of shrinking back, no "remove these evil men from office." It was only forward-moving, kingdom-first focused.

Today in our churches, particularly in the Western world, we use prayer as a fix-it tool. Make our lives better. Something comes along in someone's life that is uncomfortable, and the immediate way we pray is "get them back to status quo."

Over the past forty years or so, a huge myth about prayer has been perpetuated over and over again in our churches. Prayer is to make our life good. Unless that myth can be exposed and corrected in a congregation, it will be difficult to move forward in prayer.

SUGGESTION: An excellent resource to help leaders better understand the importance of prayer is the booklet *My House Shall Be a House of Prayer* (Navpress 2001). Besides presenting five areas in which to develop prayer, it also contains a short Bible study on prayer in the book of Acts. Just taking your leaders through this study is worth the cost of the book! You can get the booklet at prayershop.org.

.: FRUIT-BEARING PRAYER :.

If we want to see our churches truly do something for the Kingdom, and grow Kingdom-minded, Kingdom-committed followers, then we need to help shift the focus of their prayers from fix-it to fruit-bearing.

John 15 has the most amazing prayer promise in Scripture: "If you remain in me and my words remain in you, ask whatever you wish, and it will be done for you" (v. 7). It is a powerful truth, but often taken out of context.

John 15 is the illustration of Christ being the Vine, God the Father as the Gardener, and we are the branches. To be healthy branches, we have to stay attached to the Vine. We have to draw all of our sustenance for life from the Vine. We do that by reading His Word and by connecting to God in prayer.

The passage also says that our role as branches is to bear fruit. "He cuts off every branch in me that bears no fruit, while every branch that does bear fruit he prunes so that it will be even more fruitful. . . . Remain in me, as I also remain in you. No branch can bear fruit by itself; it must remain in the vine. Neither can you bear fruit unless you remain in me" (vv. 2-4).

After all of this foundation, we come to verse 7 and our prayer promise. "If you remain in me and my words remain in you . . ." we will get what we want. But if a believer is truly connected to the Vine, taking in the Word, and realizing that their primary purpose as a believer is to bear fruit, what will they want? Likely, instead of praying the possibly selfish fix-this-situation prayer, they will think, *What's the fruit-bearing thing I should ask for? What does the Vine want me to pray for? What could I pray for—for myself, this person, my church—that would bring Kingdom results, where God would get the glory and the Kingdom would grow?*

If you can encourage this one shift in prayer—helping people to understand that the primary purpose of prayer is not to make my life better—you will ultimately see radical changes in the Kingdom ministry of your church.

.: CHANGING THIS PRACTICE :.

It is not difficult to teach this principle. But it is important to continually encourage this type of Kingdom praying, because even if people learn the principle in their heads, their hearts will often take them right back to "make my life better." And it's not as if God does not want to "give good gifts to those who ask him" (Matthew 7:11).

But beyond teaching, one of the things we need to do is be careful that our actions do not perpetuate fix-it praying. And we often do that in several ways.

1. Stuck in default mode

As leaders we want to encourage and minister comfort to our people. When we are asked to pray for a need in someone's life, this "pastoral" mode often kicks in. Rather than seek direction from the Holy Spirit before praying out of default, we quickly pray for whatever the need calls for to be fixed.

Instead, we should seek to pray a meaningful, sensitive, Spirit-driven prayer that seeks what God desires to do in the situation.

2. Sameness in our practice

Because of our desire to minister in a caring way to our people, many churches (especially smaller ones) have a time to pray for needs in their worship service. Some even call for public requests before prayer is offered. Other churches have prayer ministry teams set up in the front of a church at a point in a service, and people can come up to them for personal prayer. Both are loving acts of ministry. But if those things are the only public prayer practices in your church, they perpetuate the myth that prayer is a fix-it tool.

You need variety. It is okay to do these things in a service, but make sure you have an equal amount of other prayer experiences in a service as well—experiences that teach people to pray outside of themselves and their needs.

Sameness is the easiest thing to do. Because of this, many churches always do the same thing, at the same time, service after service. If you want to move people into a more "Acts-like" experience of prayer, you can't be stuck in sameness! There are many creative ways to model praying in your services other than just covering needs in a "fix-them" way. You need to regularly have prayer that seeks Kingdom growth and God's presence instead of His hand.

.: CONCLUSION :.

It is clear that the early church prayed! It also seems clear that they focused on Kingdom growth rather than on their own comfort. As you consider how to become a praying church, one of the most significant things you can tweak is to shift from fix-it prayers to outward praying. That shift is not as hard as it might seem. Simply relooking at what public prayer practices you offer your people and pausing before you pray for someone to ask the Holy Spirit what to pray might be all you have to do.

CHAPTER 2

SIMPLE TWEAKING CAN BRING RESULTS

A FEW YEARS AGO, I was in a significant-sized church in Newton, Iowa, where I saw something that amazed me.

Scheduled to speak in both services, I was sitting in one of the front rows of the sanctuary about ten minutes prior to the first service. People were starting to gather for the service. At one point, I turned around and saw something unusual. All over the sanctuary, there were clusters of people—twos and threes—with heads bowed, arms on shoulders, praying. I had never seen spontaneous prayer quite like that before in a church.

After the service, I went into the foyer to greet people. My amazement continued as there, too, I saw clusters of people praying for each other.

Later in the day, I asked the church's prayer leader, Mark, how that came about. He told me that a while ago the lead pastor, Cory, was convicted that if he was talking to someone after church who mentioned something that could be prayed over, he should do it right then. So he started praying for his people this way. Next, he challenged his staff to do the same. He even put a little accountability in the mix by telling his staff that at staff meeting on Monday, they were to share who they prayed with the previous day. So his staff started doing this each week. His people started catching on. Because it was modeled for them, they started praying this way for others. Soon an entire congregation was ministering to each other in that manner.

A simple tweak from a senior pastor brought about a tangible improvement to the prayer atmosphere in this church. That can happen in your church as well with some simple tweaks.

.: BOLD MOVE OR SIMPLE TWEAK? :.

I have talked with a lot of prayer leaders and pastors who wanted to grow more prayer in their church throughout the twenty years I have been in prayer ministry. Many have a vision of what they would like for their church. But often that vision is way beyond what is feasible aside from a major revival hitting their church.

By the same token, I have seen a few churches take some very bold steps to try to push or drag their people into becoming a praying church. Some churches have shut down all ministries and only do prayer for a period of time—two weeks, a month, even six months. I have seen several other churches do something less drastic. They shut down every ministry one night a week—prayer meeting night—and do not allow any competing ministry to take place. While there were certainly some major blessings that came from giving more focused emphasis to prayer for a time, none of these churches saw the results they were hoping for—their people giving proper attention to prayer after the initial emphasis. Though all had taken some steps forward, most saw a stronger group of praying leaders, some improved the participation in their prayer ministries, and one saw some major directional shifts as a result of hearing God's voice.

What I am saying, however, is that if God leads you to do something drastic to get your people more active in prayer, go for it. But most churches can see results by simply tweaking where they are by improving their prayer emphasis one step at a time.

.: SOME THINGS TO CONSIDER :. FOR PASTORS

If you are a pastor, there are some things you can do to improve and tweak your prayer emphasis that a lay or staff prayer leader cannot do.

First, you probably have some clout and influence with the elder or governing board (admittedly, that is not always the case). In many churches, the biggest hindrance to seeing prayer increase is the leadership. I don't mean that there are bad people on your board who deliberately want to thwart the work of God in your church. Once in a while, however, there are such people. I had a pastor friend (who was an assistant in a more traditional church) tell me of a confrontation he once had with a leader who point-blank said, "We're tired of all this Jesus crap!" But that response is pretty unusual.

Few would argue against prayer. But many boards have individuals who do not "get" prayer. They do not see its importance in a congregation. These people respond in one of two ways:

1. They might not openly oppose an effort to increase prayer, but they will be passive-aggressive against it. Comments like "I can pray at home" or "prayer is very personal; we should not push people" will come out. They will also refuse to commit to whatever the added prayer emphasis requires of them.
2. There are people who, because of their lack of understanding, have to be coached into believing it is needed. These people will likely think everything is fine. "We are a praying church," they might respond. Once they realize that they are not as strong a praying church as they think, they will likely support you.

You will need to convince and capture the passion of the elder board and/or governing board in any effort to increase prayer significantly. Without their support, you will struggle to get the church moving to a deeper level of prayer.

SUGGESTION: One of the best resources available to help church leaders understand the importance of prayer is the sister resource to this book, *Forgotten Power: A Simple Theology of a Praying Church* by Dr. David Butts.

A relatively short book, *Forgotten Power* includes a "Points to Ponder" section with each chapter that will generate discussion among your leaders. Using this resource will teach, encourage, and challenge your leaders to move forward in prayer, and it will likely also help you discern who among your leadership does not get it, or might be outright opposition to moving forward. Very worthwhile things to know!

If your church is larger and you are more staff driven, you may need to get staff members on board with this emphasis. How do you get a youth pastor to buy in? A small groups pastor? Worship pastor? Most of the same suggestions and principles apply in trying to encourage your staff.

There is one roadblock with staff, however, that you need to consider. If you are going to push your staff to give more of their time and effort to prayer—both in their own life and in discipling the people to whom they minister—also consider by what criteria your church leadership will measure the success of your staff's ministry. What are the goals they need to meet to not risk losing their jobs? If that criteria is numerical in any way, it could be very difficult to get staff to join your efforts with much passion. For example, let's say you have a benchmark for your youth pastor that the number of kids reached would increase by ten percent this year. While that pastor should see prayer as a way to bring this about, it is also very likely that he or she will see that they have to put their energies into outreach, into making the ministry more attractive and exciting to teens. Just something to think about as you try to engage your staff in this effort to become a praying church.

So what do you tweak to get these groups to support this new emphasis? Perhaps a little discipling in prayer with your leaders is in order. Maybe a short Bible study on prayer before each meeting of the group would help. Providing some examples of what other churches are doing or how changes have affected other churches might help. A prayer retreat, where the new prayer emphasis is laid out, could help. Three books/booklets might also be good to put into the hands of your leaders. *Forgotten*

Power (PrayerShop 2015), *Living in the Upper Room* (PrayerShop 2013) and *My House Shall Be a House of Prayer* (Pray! Books 2001) can offer a very practical picture of what a praying church looks like and how to get there. They are all available at prayershop.org.

As a pastor, not only do you have some influence with the leadership, but you also are likely the biggest influencer of the congregation. You influence individuals simply because of the respect they have for you, and because of this, you exert major influence from the platform. Your congregation is watching you. What is important to the pastor becomes important to many in your congregation.

Because of that influence, there is much you can do to improve prayer, and your efforts multiply if your elder or governing board is in agreement. But it is also possible, even if your elder board does not buy into a plan to emphasize prayer growth.

.: WHAT CAN YOU DO? :.

Like Cory, a pastor in most churches has a lot of freedom to do personal ministry. You can begin praying more often for your people—especially praying in a Kingdom way, rather than in a fix-it way. Making a concerted effort to pray more over people outside of the worship service can reap benefits.

Ask yourself, What aspects of ministry am I in almost complete control over? In most churches, a pastor does not have to run his worship service agenda by the board. Could you tweak some things there that bring in more aspects of prayer, that provide more meaningful prayer experiences, that model outward praying opportunities? In the appendix of this book, I provide some practical suggestions for different prayer ideas you can apply in a worship service.

Can you start providing meaningful prayer guides for your people? Perhaps use guides that relate to your sermons or guides that encourage people to pray a Kingdom agenda for their families, their community, and so forth.

I encourage you to spend some time thinking through what you have oversight of. What tweaks can you make in those areas that will move prayer forward in some way.

.: FOR PRAYER LEADERS :.

If you are a lay prayer leader in your church, you also can be highly influential in increasing prayer in a congregation. Though you certainly do not have the clout of a pastor or elder, there still are things you can do.

Here are some key points to think about:

- What is your relationship and level of influence with your pastor and with the elder board or governing board? What is the "chain of command" between you and them?
- Do you have any control over aspects of what you do, or do any changes, ideas, etc., need to be run by them for approval?
- If you have significant influence, then there is much you can do to influence prayer. If this is your situation, pay close attention to Chapter 3 of this book, "Discipling Your People in Prayer," and Chapter 9, "Three Starting Points to Increase Prayer."
- If you do not have a lot of influence, remember that through prayer and the power of the Holy Spirit, doors can open. Continue to pray that God will show you how to influence your leadership in a godly, nonthreatening or demanding way. Pray and ask direction over the things that you do have control over. Are there some things you can set in place within your role as prayer leader that can stimulate more prayer? Can you put together good prayer guides? Can you put together a meaningful prayer weekend that is within your budget? Can you suggest a prayer initiative to your pastor or a prayer course to an adult Sunday school teacher?
- Finally, if you are in a situation where you feel that no one or few in leadership "gets" the importance of prayer, I want to encourage you not to give up. Pray! Ask God to begin to move among your leaders. Don't ever be a squeaky wheel or someone who chastises leadership.

As a person of prayer, you should be your pastor's and leaders' biggest advocate, not their most annoying critic!

.: CONCLUSION :.

Tweaking prayer can have profound results in any church. While it is great to plan (and Chapter 8, "From Tweaking to Strategy," helps you do this), simple improvements or changes can ultimately reap great rewards in prayer growth.

I know one church that wanted to bless its people by praying for their needs but also wanted its weekly prayer meeting to have a more Kingdom-focused agenda. A number of years ago it made a simple tweak.

People had always been able to write prayer requests down on a form in the bulletin on Sunday. Those requests would be prayed over by staff and in the weekly prayer gathering. Instead of focusing on lists at the prayer meeting, the church started putting these requests on little slips of paper (about 2" x 8.5"). Each slip held one request, though most weeks each request was on multiple slips of paper so more than one person had each request. Those slips were put on a stand in the entry of the sanctuary and as people came in for the prayer meeting, they picked up a slip. Many prayed for the person as they waited for the gathering to start. The prayer meeting became mostly leader led, where the leader would give prayer agendas for the people to focus on. But at a point in the gathering, people were asked to take out their slips, come to the altar, hold up their slips, and pray out loud—all at once—for the need on their slip. (Some prayed silently.) A very powerful incense rose to the throne of God!

This approach accomplished a number of things. The requests no longer dominated the prayer meeting, people were blessed and felt their requests were prayed for effectively, and the church was able to focus most of the prayer time on a greater Kingdom agenda.

A simple tweak.

CHAPTER 3

DISCIPLING YOUR PEOPLE IN PRAYER

A NUMBER OF YEARS AGO, I was an elder in a church. I recall one elders' meeting where, at the start of the meeting, our pastor encouraged us to pray for areas of spiritual need in our lives or in the congregation. I was shocked at the response; only the pastor and I followed the instructions. The other elders all prayed for some kind of physical need—one his mother-in-law's health, the others for similar health issues in their families. I thought the directions were pretty clear, so I wondered why they were unable to pray about spiritual needs.

Some time later, our pastor encouraged this same group to come to a weekly early morning prayer time (we opened it to others in the church as well). The focus would be on God's moving in our midst and the power of His Spirit being unleashed among us. I was in!

The first week, seven or eight people came. The pastor re-emphasized the focus. For about thirty minutes, we stayed on task. Then, someone prayed for our troops (we had just gone into Afghanistan). Nothing was said about the focus shift. The next week, we stayed on task for about fifteen minutes before people started praying their own agendas. Again, nothing was said. The third week, we started "off topic" right away. Within a few more weeks, the prayer meeting began to dissolve as people stopped coming.

As I thought back on those things, it was clear that many of those people had never been discipled into prayer beyond simple petition or intercession for our immediate needs. They either simply did not have the tools to pray beyond simple "fix-it" prayers, or they had an insufficient understanding of why one would pray for something beyond that.

.: DISCIPLESHIP IGNORED :.

When I grew up (1960s-1980s), there was a huge emphasis on discipleship in the Church. Resources and emphasis on Bible knowledge were significant. Churches taught the Bible multiple times during the week, in different settings. It was during this era that many churches in the West abandoned their weekly prayer meetings in favor of "Family Night," where they had a full program for all ages to gain Bible knowledge. I am amazed that we did not see better results from that in the Church.

But in almost all churches, one key area of discipleship was totally ignored: prayer. There was very little discipleship in prayer. I think it was assumed that prayer development would happen naturally. "Prayer is caught, not taught" was a popular phrase. Yet churches offered few places for it to be caught!

Development in prayer does not happen naturally in most people. It needs to be both caught and taught. Churches that recognize this will begin to look for ways to disciple their people in prayer at all levels.

Here are some key things to consider as you seek to better disciple your people.

1. We pray what we know.

From the youngest child to the oldest adult, we usually cannot pray out of our sphere of knowledge. Certainly there are times where the Spirit really takes over as we pray and provides us with additional knowledge and words, but that is not the norm in most people's prayer lives.

When a parent is teaching a young child how to pray, the child usually prays for Mommy, Daddy, siblings, grandparents, pets—things that are in their immediate area of knowledge. But then they might add a friend, a neighbor, a pastor. Sunday school teachers or parents add a friend who doesn't know Jesus to their list—maybe a nation of the world or a missionary.

Adults are like this too. When we start praying as a new believer, we start with our immediate sphere of knowledge too—our needs (petition). If we are not taught to pray beyond that, we do not progress. To change this, adults need to put themselves in places where they hear other things being prayed for (intercession, spiritual growth, spiritual warfare).

It is by hearing someone in church pray for a nation or community transformation, that they will begin to add those things. This all comes from discipleship.

Can you see what happens if the only prayer time a church ever has in a worship service is always focused on people's needs? They will grow believers who think that is all prayer is for—"fix my life."

Church leaders need to look for ways to enlarge their people's prayer agenda and experiences. That should be a part of the planned discipleship agenda of a church. Church Christian Education people need to make it a part of planning and they need to help teachers understand how to teach praying beyond felt needs in their classes. Youth leaders and men's and women's group leaders need to do the same.

2. We all pray differently.

One of the things that needs to be better understood in prayer discipleship is that we all do not pray the same way. Our personalities and character traits and our spiritual gifts shape the way we pray.

For example, a person with the spiritual gift of helps or mercy may get excited praying for the needs of people. They will come to a prayer time that is focused on members' needs. But a person with a gift of evangelism will be bored to tears in such a prayer meeting. He or she wants to pray for the lost and for community transformation.

A person with pessimistic tendencies will pray differently than an optimist. The pessimist is likely to name every problem; the optimist is likely to pray blessing over a situation. We need both views!

And then there is the fact that God gives many people a specific burden in prayer. Some in your congregation will eventually have a burden to pray for children, for their pastor, for the nation, for a missionary, and so on.

I regularly speak in churches, doing seminars on prayer. But I seldom teach a seminar that is highly focused on one prayer practice—like journaling, for example. Why? Because a seminar on journaling will only speak to a narrow group of people—those who like to write and who value writing down what they sense God saying to them. I try to teach broader principles that will bless everyone, but that is hard to do.

Churches that "cookie cutter" prayer will only bless a few people.

A church that wants to disciple its people well in prayer will consider this truth and will do public prayer in a variety of ways. It will look for ways to stimulate prayer burdens and provide an outlet for prayer release and accommodate the varied personalities of its members.

Some in your congregation will value prayer as relationship, while others will be intercessors who believe prayer releases the will of God and expands His kingdom.

The problem with all of this is twofold. First you will have issues with people who insist that their style or burden should be everyone's. They may insist that we all need to pray for missions, for example. Or that everyone needs to focus on having thirty minutes of prayer first thing in the morning. Second, it can be a challenge for church leaders to provide a prayer experience or topic that is meaningful for everyone.

The first problem can simply be solved with gentle correction. The second problem is ongoing, but a church can handle it effectively if they simply remember the truth and do not always do prayer the same way. Shake it up in your morning worship services. Make an effort to put various prayer opportunities in front of your people. Provide information on various days of prayer or make prayer guides on different subjects available to your people.

3. Teach Praying Scripture.

While there are lots of ways to pray, I personally believe the absolute bedrock method of prayer that everyone should learn—even if it doesn't become a primary method for them—is to pray Scripture. Every person in our pews needs to learn how to take a verse of Scripture and turn it back into a prayer to the Father.

This is highly important for several reasons. First, we know we need to pray God's will if we are going to see answers. Praying God's will is not always easy, especially when we do not know what God's will is in a situation. But we also know that what is in God's Word is God's will! If I can pray a verse over a situation when I know that verse is God's will, then my faith and expectation rises.

Second, it will get your men praying more effectively. One of the biggest hindrances to prayer in men is that they do not know what to say. Men are typically less verbal than women. I know that is a generalization, but it is largely true. I find that fewer men than women will pray in public. If you teach men to pray Scripture, this will not happen. Men are given a language to use when they pray out loud. You will see results.

Third, it will encourage people to move away from fix-it prayers to prayers that seek God's heart and purposes over situations. It is harder to make specific requests that tell God what to do when you are praying His Word back to Him.

SUGGESTION: There are some wonderful resources currently available that can help you disciple your people in praying Scripture. Any are good, but here are a few we suggest.

1. *Solid Foundation* booklet. This 48-page, 4" x 6" booklet both inspires the reader as to the importance of praying Scripture and specifically shows them how to take a verse and pray it. Individual copies are $2.99, but if you shop at our store, prayershop.org, we have multiple copy discounts that make it very inexpensive for a church. 100 or more copies are only .59 each.

2. *Pray the Word* products. The *Pray the Word* line presents powerful Scripture-based prayers for individuals to pray through. What is unique about these books compared to other Scripture-prayer products is that the prayers are designed to make people pray beyond just reciting the prayer, and the prayers are very much focused on heart issues, not on fix-it needs. *Pray the Word for Your Church* also includes a 21-page journal that encourages people to pray specific Scriptures God gives them over the various ministries of their church. Again, multiple copy discounts are available at prayershop.org.

4. Theology They Need.

A lot of people in our pews struggle because they do not have a good theology of prayer. They do not understand how prayer works, how they should engage in it, and many have little expectation that it will work.

People need to be discipled effectively to understand the two primary purposes for prayer:

1. Prayer grows a personal relationship with God.
2. Prayer releases the will of God on earth.

Whether you are theologically from a Calvinist or Arminian background, you need to explain those two purposes in your theological bent and jargon.

First, people need to understand the importance of prayer in growing their relationship with God. Prayer is the avenue for us to know God personally. When we have a prayer life (no matter if it is a struggling one or a satisfying one), we have a point of connection with God. As a result, God is able to conform us to His image. He works in our hearts to shape us and mold us. He changes our hearts when we pray, to align us with what He wants to do. When a believer does not have a prayer life he or she is working on, God seems less active in their life. Encouraging people to develop their prayer relationship with God will make them good parishioners, eager to see the kingdom grow in and through their church.

The second point is also very important if you want to see your church members active in the Kingdom. No one will pray for much outside their own personal needs if they do not understand that their prayers are a part of moving the hand of God. A church that teaches its people this principle will see Kingdom results.

One of my favorite passages of Scripture that helps us to understand this truth is 2 Corinthians 1:8-11.

> We do not want you to be uninformed, brothers and sisters, about the troubles we experienced in the province of Asia. We were under great pressure, far beyond our

> ability to endure, so that we despaired of life itself. Indeed, we felt we had received the sentence of death. But this happened that we might not rely on ourselves but on God, who raises the dead. He has delivered us from such a deadly peril, and he will deliver us again. On him we have set our hope that he will continue to deliver us, as you help us by your prayers. Then many will give thanks on our behalf for the gracious favor granted us in answer to the prayers of many.

I don't think this was a missionary writing to his supporting churches at the end of the year saying, "We had a tough year, but thanks for praying. We were encouraged just knowing people were praying." No. Paul literally believed it was the prayers of the Corinthian believers that thwarted Satan enough that they could keep moving forward on this journey. I believe this teaches the truth that when you pray for a ministry or missionary, in the heavenly scheme of things, your prayers are just as important to the success or failure of a ministry as the missionary on the front lines. Paul challenged the Roman believers to "join me in my struggle by praying to God for me" (Romans 15:30). This was not just an encouragement or a camaraderie reason to pray—it had a spiritual effect.

A word to Calvinists here: Notice I did not say prayer **dictates** the will of God; it releases it. When we pray what is on God's heart, what He puts within our hearts to pray, it happens! And that is how He uses us to grow the Kingdom.

I like to use this illustration to help explain it: Imagine a picture of a hand opening representing God's will being released. Our prayers are like the muscles and tendons in the arm. But God is the brain. What's opening the hand? The brain sends impulses to the arm so the muscles and tendons move in a way that opens the hand.

That is the wonderful way God uses us to help grow His Kingdom. When people begin to understand this fact that moves them deeper into intercession. That is a sign of maturing spiritually.

An understanding of both principles (personal relationship and release of God's will) is crucial to disciple a person into effective prayer. Those two principles work together. As we grow in relationship, we get a greater desire to pray what is on God's heart, rather than what we want. The more Christlike we become, the quicker our heart—and what we pray—seeks to pray what will grow the Kingdom.

.: CONCLUSION :.

Any church that wants to become a prayer force needs to consider how it can better disciple its people in prayer. Focusing on these four areas will begin to develop your congregation into not only a strong praying force but will make them better Kingdom-minded believers in the process.

CHAPTER 4

..‖ THE BENEFITS OF PRAYING TOGETHER ‖..

I WAS RECENTLY IN A SMALL CHURCH that for years has struggled to grow beyond sixty people. They are dear, sincere people who want to trust God to use them in greater ways in their community. I challenged them to focus more on Kingdom issues in their prayers (as opposed to just the needs of the congregation).

In a Facebook chat a few weeks later, the pastor's wife commented that they had tweaked the way they were praying, and a neighbor had prayed to receive Christ that week. A month after this they saw six women pray to receive Christ at a women's event. I will continue to pray for a renewed passion to seek the kingdom as they pray together.

Despite the fact that many churches do not have significant corporate prayer expressions, most prayer leaders and pastors believe praying together is important. But what are the benefits? There are many benefits, but here are three significant ones.

1. Praying together invites the presence and power of the Holy Spirit.

In 2 Chronicles 6-7, we see the dedication of Solomon's Temple. While "the whole assembly of Israel was standing there" (2 Chron. 6:3), Solomon prays a dedicatory prayer in which he invokes the presence of God. "Now, my God, may your eyes be open and your ears attentive to the prayers offered in this place. Now arise, O LORD God, and come to your resting place, you and the ark of your might. May your priests, O LORD God, be clothed with salvation, may your saints rejoice in your goodness" (6:40-

41). Of course the presence of God entered with dynamic power!

There is a different atmosphere in churches that pray together and who have praying people. Worship seems more powerful. There is a sense of connection with God that is not there in non-praying churches.

A few years ago, I held a conference at a church in Michigan. The church had invited many other churches to attend the conference and they had responded—more than 300 were in attendance. As these people (hungry people who wanted to grow closer to God through prayer) worshiped and prayed together, something happened. God showed up! There were multiple times where we so sensed His presence that we had to just be silent for seemingly long stretches of time (up to five minutes).

A number of years ago at our prayer leaders' convention, Dr. Tommy Barnett, pastor of First Assembly of God Church in Phoenix, Arizona, said, "The presence of God in the midst of a church is directly proportional to the amount of prayer that takes place there."

When the Spirit of God is manifestly present, other things happen. People hear Him speak, giving direction and encouragement. The church in Antioch saw this truth in action: "While they were worshiping the Lord and fasting, the Holy Spirit said, 'Set apart for me Barnabas and Saul for the work to which I have called them.' So after they had fasted and prayed, they placed their hands on them and sent them off" (Acts 13:2-3). During a normal time of prayer and worship, the Holy Spirit gave crucial direction that forever changed the world—Saul (Paul) began his missionary work.

As you pray together as a congregation, God will begin to "show up" more and more.

2. Praying together increases the faith of a congregation to believe God for the miraculous.

Matthew 17 and Mark 9 tell the story of a father who brought his demon-possessed son to the disciples. They could not cast the demon out. The boy was taken to Jesus, who issued a simple command and the demon left. Later, the disciples came to Jesus and they were baffled. Why? Because they knew how to cast out demons. (The story takes place after they had been sent two by two into villages casting out demons and healing the sick.) They asked Jesus why they couldn't do it.

Jesus said two things: "because you have so little faith" (Matthew 17:20), and "this kind can come out only by prayer" (Mark 9:29). I wonder if the disciples attacked this demon issue cavalierly or routinely. They knew the words to say, the steps to take. But nothing worked because they were not prayed up enough. Their faith was not there as a result. There is a clear connection between prayer and faith (beyond the fact that we are supposed to pray in faith).

I believe the most significant thing that is lost in a church that does not have corporate prayer is faith. There is simply no expectation that God will do the miraculous. One of the main reasons most churches are stagnant and do not see God at work in miraculous ways in their midst is that most churches and individuals do not know what it is to pray in faith anymore. But faith grows as we pray together.

Here's how it works: Maybe I personally am going through a tough time. In the midst of it, I try to pray with trust and faith, but it is difficult because I only see the issue. If I go and pray with others, however, what happens? As I listen to others pray with more faith than I have, my faith grows. Here's how it works in a corporate situation. Let's say our church is planning to build a new facility, and we feel it is God's will for us to do so. But I'm an elder who is skeptical of the plans because they are beyond what we can afford to do. I begin to pray with others regarding this. God can now put a heart of trust in me, He can bring me to unity with others, He can give me the faith to believe Him for the miraculous—His vision and plan for my church. When I only pray by myself, that is less likely to happen.

Churches that do not pray together still minister in whatever ways they can, given their resources, abilities, and sacrifices. But churches that pray together begin to see the miraculous power of God at work in their midst. It goes beyond what they can and should do into what God wants to do through them.

A few years ago, our ministry's founder, Dave Butts, shared on becoming a praying church at a pastor and elder gathering at Lincoln College in Illinois. A number of leaders from Northpoint Church near St. Louis were there. A year or so after his presentation, Dave received an email from its prayer leader. In it, he shared what God had been doing in their church since the gathering. In March of 2009, Northpoint was not growing and its budget was $40,000 in the red. Dave's message inspired these leaders to encourage and challenge their people to come out to their Sunday morning prayer times. The prayer meeting grew in number of attendees. They focused prayer on God's blessing, asking that His transformational power would once again move Northpoint forward. They put forth a prayer challenge called "750 in the Black," meaning they wanted to grow to more than 750 attendees and be financially in the black. Less than a year after increasing the prayers, they were well in the black and more than 700 were coming to services each week.

If you increase the level of praying together among your congregation, you will see more miracles happen as your faith rises.

3. Praying together moves people from seeking their own purposes to desiring God's purposes.

Most people's prayers seek the best fix for a situation. We typically pray whatever we are told to pray for a situation, with no real thought of "What does God want to do here?" Something happens to that dynamic, however, when people pray together. They start to let go of their desires to see their purposes fulfilled and start to open themselves up to what God wants.

The value of this to a church is huge when it comes to ministry and decision making. If people pray together over an issue, even if people come to prayer thinking they know what the church should do, praying together opens them up to God's desire.

Years ago, I was a part of a church plant in Colorado Springs that was meeting in a school. We felt the Lord leading us to purchase land. We found two pieces of property—one was very close to the school and forty-two of our families, the other was three to four miles away. That distance was not a big deal, but it was not in the neighborhood we had been ministering in for the past five years. The property close to us cost 1.5 million, the other $450,000. Many of us felt the issue was not the difference in price, but where God wanted us. Pray, figure that out, and He will provide. There were leaders on both sides of which piece to purchase. We started praying together. We even called a corporate prayer meeting on one of the pieces of property. As we did that, God began to put a vision of the ministry we could have on the $450,000 piece of property into those of us who wanted the other property. That is what God will do when we pray together—agreement comes so we can pray His will with confidence.

People who are disgruntled with decisions a church has made usually have not prayed with the body over that issue. Pray together and watch unity grow.

.: THE CHALLENGE :.

Jeremiah 29:11-13 is a powerful promise written to a corporate body of people. "'For I know the plans I have for you,' declares the LORD, 'plans to prosper you and not to harm you, plans to give you hope and a future. Then you will call upon me and come and pray to me, and I will listen to you. You will seek me and find me when you seek me with all your heart.'"

The "all" there is numeric—God is saying if all of you would seek me, you will find the plans I have for you. If we want to see God's blessing in our churches, if we want to see Jesus' transforming power, the dynamic ministry of the Holy Spirit in our midst, then we need to pray together.

In this day and age, it is very difficult to get people to commit to more nights at a church. Many churches have stopped holding weekly prayer meetings. But these benefits suggest that churches need to reconsider providing opportunities for corporate prayer.

As leaders, seek the Lord as to what to tweak to make more praying together happen in your church. If you already have a weekly prayer meeting with more than a few attending, perhaps some tweaks to make it more dynamic will help. Then promote the meeting. There are people in most congregations who would attend a midweek prayer meeting if they were taught why it was important to the life of a church, and if they were regularly encouraged to go.

But, if you do not have something you can tweak—or if the prayer meeting is beyond tweaking—I encourage you to consider where you can add prayer to existing gatherings where most of your people already are. The worship service is a primary place to include more dynamic times of prayer. See Chapter 6, "Prayer in the Worship Service" for ideas. If you have a strong adult Sunday school program or a very active small group ministry, this can work too—though in small groups, because of their nature, it is very difficult to move people to pray beyond the needs of just the people in the group.

Also, remember that you can have powerful corporate prayer on a smaller corporate level. What do I mean by that? When all your elders meet, their prayers for church-related issues are powerful because of their authority over the church. If all your Sunday school teachers meet together and pray over the ministry of the Sunday school, there is a powerful corporate nature to that. By encouraging additional "Spirit-empowering prayer" among the leaders of different areas of ministry, powerful things will happen as a result.

CHAPTER 5

BIBLICAL PRINCIPLES OF CORPORATE PRAYER

A NUMBER OF YEARS AGO, I was preparing to go to California to facilitate a prayer weekend in a Presbyterian church there. I had been planning the event with their prayer leader and his committee. As we planned, the committee felt that it would be great to have me lead a prayer time in the two morning worship services. They had never really experienced a time where anyone other than a person from the platform prayed in the service.

This would be an event where I would guide people to pray in groups on a theme. It would be a stretch for their staid people. They presented the idea to their pastor. He balked. "We can't make people feel uncomfortable like that," he surmised. He and I talked through what I would do. No one would be forced to pray; I would put some prayer points and a sample prayer on a PowerPoint slide; it would only go three to four minutes. He finally allowed it.

Even though we were nervous as to how people would respond, it went off fabulously well. People prayed. I remember standing on the platform during each service (with about 400 people or so in each) and listening to a glorious din of voices rising out of that beautiful sanctuary. During the second service, I even had a vision while they were praying (something that had only happened to me once before). I told the congregation later that I saw their new multipurpose building filled with people and many people responding to the gospel there. I said, "I don't know what that means, but watch."

The pastor got nothing but positive comments afterward: "that was so dynamic," "I have never prayed in public before," and "we have to do that again." They started regularly doing prayer times like that in their services. And the vision? The prayer leader emailed me about nine months later. They had planned to do an outreach event with a Christian magician in their multipurpose building. So many people bought tickets that they had to schedule a second "show." Dozens responded to the gospel that weekend through the events.

Why was the response so significant? Because the prayer time was not the typical prayer most of us are used to—focused on fix-it needs that have little relation to God's Kingdom purposes.

You can tweak the way you do prayer without too many people even noticing. And if you develop prayer that focuses outwardly and that utilizes scriptural principles of corporate prayer, you will see your people get on board.

.: BIBLICAL PRINCIPLES :.

There are five biblical principles of powerful corporate prayer. The more these elements are present in our prayer times (during worship or other times), the more powerful the prayer.

1. Desperation

Ezra records a time of corporate prayer surrounding a three-day fast. The priest Ezra was taking a group of Jews back to repopulate Israel. They were going to cross dangerous terrain and needed protection.

> There, by the Ahava Canal, I proclaimed a fast, so that we might humble ourselves before our God and ask him for a safe journey for us and our children, with all our possessions. I was ashamed to ask the king for soldiers and horsemen to protect us from enemies on the road, because we had told the king, "The gracious hand of our God is on everyone who looks to him, but his great anger is against all who forsake him." So we fasted and petitioned our God about this, and he answered our prayer. (Ezra 8:21-23)

They prayed out of desperation. They were in trouble if God did not come through. The interesting thing, however, is that Ezra had a solution: Ask the king for soldiers to go along. From the pages of Ezra, we see he had a good relationship with the king. The king had given them permission to go. But Ezra refused to ask the king for protection. He refused to do the obvious thing in favor of relying on God.

We need to learn from that. The more desperate we are about something, the more vibrant our prayers will be. When you are going to pray corporately, look for ways to impress a sense of desperation in your people. Remember what happened in churches following 9/11? Prayer meetings were full for several weeks. Why? Desperation.

We will see corporate prayer become more dynamic—and have greater participation—if our focus is about something with a measure of desperation in it. When you plan the prayer focus, figure out a way to build in desperation. Is there something happening in the world or in your city that has people's attention and the people have no control over? Pray about that. When you can pray, "we can't solve this, God; we need You," you will see more people participate and their prayers will be filled with greater passion.

2. One Focus

Powerful prayer is focused prayer. It is not a shotgun approach—giving prayer requests and praying for ten different things. Effective corporate prayer is topical. The leader explains, "Now we are going to pray for . . ."

We see this played out in the story of Peter's imprisonment (Acts 12). Verse 5 tells us "so Peter was kept in prison, but the church was earnestly praying to God for him." This obviously was a very focused prayer meeting! They did not take requests and pray for everything under the sun. No "Martha, how is that back of yours? How can we pray?" and then "Oh yeah, don't forget Peter. Who's got an update on Peter? He's still in prison, isn't he? Let's remember Peter."

One of the ways over the years that the church has severely weakened corporate prayer is that we let prayer be about the people there, rather than about God. We allowed prayer to focus on every little fix-it need of those in attendance and ignored the Kingdom advance of God. As pastor/prayer leader Daniel Henderson describes, we have made prayer horizontal rather than vertical.

That kind of prayer is dull and no one really wants to be there. In any prayer gathering, it is far more dynamic to let a leader pick a focus and stick to it. As soon as you give up leadership to everyone's agenda, you lose the dynamic nature of corporate prayer.

Especially if you are having a prayer time in the morning worship service, you should pick only one subject for which to pray. That will be far more powerful than opening it up to requests.

SUGGESTION: Bar none, this is the most significant thing you can change in a prayer gathering to make it more dynamic. Narrowing the focus and being leader-led and not letting those there take over the prayer meeting with their personal agendas will reap great rewards. I recommend three resources to you to help you develop more dynamic prayer gatherings.

1. *Fresh Encounters* (NavPress) by Daniel Henderson will teach you how to have a worship-based prayer meeting that is focused upward on Jesus, rather than on the personal needs of those in attendance.

2. *And the Place Was Shaken* (Broadman & Holman) by John Franklin gives great insight to a leader about how to handle the dynamics of leading a prayer meeting. Both books are available through prayershop.org.

3. *Fresh Prayer* by Steve Hawthorne is an online resource that provides a Scripture passage to pray through at a prayer gathering. It provides questions and suggestions for a leader to use the passage effectively. *Fresh Prayer* is available at waymakers.org.

3. One Voice

Another powerful principle about corporate prayer is the "one voice" principle. And that is a numerical principle. As was mentioned above, the same story of Peter in Acts tells us that the church was earnestly and constantly praying to God. Everyone. Not five people in a little room on Wednesday night. A powerful dynamic occurs when an entire congregation prays on the same theme.

That principle is why all-church prayer initiatives are a great practice. A prayer initiative is where the entire church prays on one theme for a set period of time—usually a week or thirty or forty days. Usually they use prayer guides that get everyone praying with the same focus. (See Chapter 9, "Three Starting Points to Increase Prayer" for more information on prayer initiatives.)

If you want to have the one-voice principle in your church, make prayer accessible in those places where you have the most people gathered. The primary place you will have the entire congregation together is Sunday morning worship. While I think the morning worship service is the most significant place to develop times of corporate prayer, there are other ways to see the one-voice principle at work.

Look for places where everyone in a given ministry is gathered. A church board meeting, an elders meeting, a Sunday school teachers meeting, youth ministry leaders, worship participants gathering, etc. In any one of these gatherings, one-voice prayer can take place. If that group prays for the Kingdom purposes of that group—what ministry areas are under its authority—then they are calling out with one voice for those areas of ministry. But alas, even when those groups get together, when they add a prayer time to their meeting, it is usually focused on the needs of those in the ministry. If that would stop, and they would focus on the Kingdom purposes of that ministry, something very dynamic would happen!

4. Invoking the Presence

In 2 Chronicles 6-7 at the dedication of Solomon's Temple, we see God's glory indwelling His Temple so much that everyone fell with their faces to the ground in humble submission and awe. No one went inside. In Solomon's dedication prayer, he invited God to come and dwell.

> "Now, my God, may your eyes be open and your ears attentive to the prayers offered in this place.
>
> "Now arise, Lord God, and come to your resting place,
> you and the ark of your might.
> May your priests, Lord God, be clothed with salvation,
> may your faithful people rejoice in your goodness."
> (2 Chronicles 6:40-41)

When we think of the presence of God, we often just take comfort in the presence spoken of in Matthew 18:20: "Where two or three are gathered together in My name, I am there in the midst of them." But there is another presence of God—what old-time Puritans used to call "His manifest presence." That is a presence you can literally sense. It is a transforming presence.

That is the presence Solomon invoked to come into the Temple. We need to look for ways to encourage that presence of God into our midst as well. He comes by invitation, and He comes through praise. Psalm 22:3 tells us that God inhabits the praises of His people.

There is no better place to regularly experience the manifest presence of God than the worship service. When we pray in the middle of or following a time of intense worship—worship that is entirely focused upward on Jesus Christ rather than on us—we more readily sense His presence, and our prayers become more Kingdom focused. Why? Because when we see God for who He really is, our needs pale in comparison. We become inspired to focus on His purposes and Kingdom.

By the same principle, if you want to see the passion and intensity of the prayers increase in weekly prayer gatherings that are held outside the morning worship service, add worship that is focused on Jesus Christ.

5. Agreement

The last element of powerful corporate prayer is praying in agreement. Agreement is different than focus. It happens when everyone knows and agrees with what they are asking God. Often when a congregation prays about an issue in a church, there is not agreement. We all have a different idea of what should be done. So when we pray, we often just pray our own agendas.

In a leader-directed prayer time during a morning worship service, it is easier to be in agreement. The leader simply gives direction as to what they will ask God to do. (There is more explanation on this in the next chapter.)

.: BRINGING IT ALL TOGETHER :.

So how do all of these work in a prayer gathering?

Let's say you have a situation where God is really blessing your congregation with growth. More and more people are coming to church; you are starting to pack your facilities out. Your leadership knows that you need to do something to allow for this growth, but what? You decide to seek the Lord for His direction. In fact, you decide you need to get everyone praying about this issue. So you call for special times of prayer, including an all-church prayer meeting.

At that prayer meeting, you have a sense of desperation because you have acknowledged you do not know what to do. You need God's wisdom and direction. You will have one focus. The prayer meeting you call everyone to will not be open to requests or other prayer needs. You will only focus on direction. You will have one voice. Because of the nature of the subject, I suspect most of your congregation will attend—many not because they want to pray, but because they are curious about what others think. But that's okay. God can work despite mixed motives. You have a time of worship and you invite the Holy Spirit to come in, to guide and direct your prayers, to reveal His will.

But you won't have agreement—at least not at the start. Why? Because many will come already knowing what you should do. Some think you should go to two services. Another will think you should plant a daughter church. Still others, rent the empty department store building down the street. No agreement.

But here is what will happen: Agreement will come in any issue if people pray together. As we pray with others, we become more open to God's agenda and let go of our own. People at that prayer meeting will begin to let go of their idea as they pray and start sensing what God truly wants to do. Agreement will come as you pray. By the same token, if you have an intense issue in your church that you are praying about, and you reach a decision, I can just about guarantee that those who criticize the decision did not pray with the body about it!

I already shared about the two pieces of property my church in Colorado Springs was wrestling over. We did not get in agreement as to which one until we began praying together. God miraculously changed the hearts of those of us who wanted the "other" property and caused us to desire the property He had for us.

.: CONCLUSION :.

Having dynamic prayer times that focus on Kingdom advancement will revolutionize your congregation. People will feel more passion and a stronger desire to pray if you work at developing these spiritual principles of corporate prayer. Fringe people and those who don't view the Christian life much beyond "what's in it for me" will be impacted spiritually. And you will begin to see greater and greater areas of transformation in people's lives, in your church, and in the community.

CHAPTER 6

..‖ PRAYER IN THE WORSHIP SERVICE ‖..

A NUMBER OF YEARS AGO, I was conducting a prayer weekend in a church in Pennsylvania. I was teaching a Friday night and Saturday seminar event for its people and preaching on Sunday morning. The pastor and I had talked about me leading a five-minute prayer time in the service where we would get people praying in groups (something new for the church). I planned for an outreach-type prayer agenda focusing on the community.

But something happened. On Saturday night, the pastor called me and told me of a tragedy that would affect his people. This church had a ministry to their local neighborhood police station. They prayed for the officers and their families, gave gifts, and did acts of kindness for them. One of the officers there had been killed in the line of duty.

I told the pastor that we needed to change the focus of our prayer time to that loss, and he needed to lead it. We talked about some prayer points and came up with the new plan.

The next morning when the prayer time came, that church exploded in voices raised to the heavenlies. I was in the front row, but I turned and prayed with an older couple, probably in their seventies. Both of them prayed out loud, multiple times in the expanded to almost ten-minute prayer time. Later the pastor told me that he had never known either of the two individuals I prayed with to pray out loud in church! They overcame their fear and prayed because they were engaged with the topic.

.: ENGAGING YOUR CONGREGATION :.

The early church in Acts did four things when it gathered together. "They continued steadfastly in the apostles' doctrine and fellowship, in the breaking of bread and in prayer" (Acts 2:42). I don't think that means 25 percent of the time was given to each activity, but it clearly shows importance was put on each element. If our church gatherings were measured against those four things, where would we stand?

Clearly, corporate prayer was given a significant place in early church meetings. Today, most churches relegate prayer to a pastor or leader praying once or twice in a service, maybe a worship leader offering a simple prayer amidst a song set, or perhaps there is a time for people to come forward and be prayed for. While these are important expressions of prayer, they do not usually constitute powerful, corporate prayer.

Instead, corporate prayer has been relegated to the weekly prayer meeting, which is certainly an important service and event for a church. Unfortunately, many churches have disbanded these due to lack of interest or due to sheer boredom. Most prayer meetings have become a few people sitting around in a circle, taking requests about the physical and personal needs of the church's members, then praying until each one has been mentioned. It is hardly a dynamic time of powerful corporate prayer.

Congregations need to experience powerful, dynamic, earth-changing corporate prayer. And the best place to experience it is in the Sunday morning worship service. Why? Three reasons:

1. Prayer is not truly corporate unless it is done with all your people. The morning worship is the only place where you have most of your people each week. As was previously mentioned, the Acts 12:5 story reminds us that "Peter was therefore kept in prison, but constant prayer was offered to God for him by the church." We can have good times of people praying together at other moments, but the value of an entire congregation calling out to God in agreement is extremely powerful. When a congregation agrees on something and prays, it is effective!

2. It teaches your people how to pray. These days, a majority of believers never participates in times of praying with others. They may observe prayer a few times in a worship service, but they are never required to try it. As a result, many believers do not have any confidence to pray. When they can see and hear others pray, that can grow their own prayer lives as well.
3. It is easier to have a leader-led prayer time in the morning worship service than at a less formal weeknight meeting. This is important for prayer to be truly effective. In the midweek prayer meeting, oftentimes well-meaning pray-ers will take the prayer meeting away from a leader to pray about their own agendas. This will not happen in a worship service.

As a result, you can better manage prayer to operate within the biblical principles of corporate prayer. In a leader-directed prayer time during a morning worship service, it is easier to be in agreement. The leader simply gives direction as to what they will ask God to do. He might say something like this: "After seeking God, the leaders of our church feel that God is moving us to look for a piece of property on which to build. Let's ask God to reveal that piece of land to us."

.: WAYS TO INCORPORATE PRAYER IN THE SERVICE :.

When incorporating group prayer into the morning worship service, several principles are important.

1. Until your people are used to it, keep it fairly short. Never let them go more than five minutes in a prayer group on one topic. Two to three minutes is plenty.
2. Put prayer points and even a simple prayer on the audiovisual screen or in the bulletin. Instruct those who are nervous about joining in that they are not being

forced to pray, but if they would like to, you've provided a prayer or some thoughts to use when they pray.

3. When you start doing this, and perhaps a few times afterward, give them some prayer protocol instructions. Remind them that they should not pray like they do when they are by themselves. All prayers should be short, thirty to forty-five seconds maximum, to give everyone a chance to participate and so no one is intimidated. People can pray multiple times in a group.

Some of you pastors may be thinking, *Our church has lots of visitors, many of whom are not yet believers. I can't make people pray in groups in that setting.* Sorry pastor, but you are completely wrong. I had a megachurch pastor who regularly led times of prayer in his morning services tell me, "Unbelievers who come to church know churches pray. They expect it. If you make it easy for them, they are not put out if you ask them to participate." Also, a few years ago I was leading a prayer gathering in a small church, where an unsaved friend of one of the teens came with her friend. She was so touched by the presence of God during a prayer time that the believing friend and her mother led this girl to Christ right during the prayer time. Provide people the opportunity to participate in times of connecting with God in a service, and you will be amazed at the results.

Here are some practical ways to incorporate prayer in a worship service setting.

1. Pray the Thoughts of a Song.

Many songs—especially contemporary ones—are prayers themselves, focused on Christ. If we mean what we are singing, then we are praying when we sing. But, another benefit is that songs can be catalysts to dynamic prayer.

For example, a song like "Touching Heaven, Changing Earth" can foster a time of prayer for revival. A song like "Breathe" can generate prayer for spiritual hunger. A song like "Crown Him with Many Crowns" or "O for a Thousand Tongues to Sing" can move us into times of corporate praise where we spontaneously shout out praises to God. A song like "God of This City" can move into a powerful time of praying for our community.

To do it, a worship leader simply guides people into groups of three to six and instructs them on what to pray. The musicians keep playing to provide some background music. After two to three minutes, end the time by moving into the next song.

If a worship leader struggles to know what to do, you can teach him or her how. Perhaps suggest a prayer topic that is fitting for some of the songs you regularly do. If the worship leader is uncomfortable, the first time or two have the pastor or a prayer leader who is comfortable quietly come up to the platform as you near the point in the song when you will go into prayer, and have them lead the congregation.

2. Set Aside a Three- to Five- Minute Prayer Time.

Pick a topic of importance to your church or leaders: an upcoming outreach event, a special program, a deep need in the church, the nation, etc. The more the topic relates to something your congregation is concerned with (such as the sudden death of the police officer in the earlier example), the more dynamic the time will be. Have people pray in groups over this topic. But again, offer clear direction and ideas of things to pray. Don't leave your people scrambling for thoughts to pray. Mature pray-ers will expand on the prayer points you give them, and less confident people will happily stick to the prayer points you provide.

As your people get used to praying in the service, you can expand the time if a special topic calls for that to happen or if it is apparent that your people are very engaged in the prayer time.

3. Have Open-Microphone Praying.

Another possible prayer opportunity is to place a live microphone on the floor in front of the platform. At a point in the service, you can use it in one of two ways. Have two to four people selected to pray from the microphone on a given topic. Let people know that you have selected people to pray and the microphone is not open for anyone. This is a powerful way for your congregation to hear how different people pray over the same issue.

If you get brave enough, you might have a time where the microphone is open to anyone who wants to pray. A worship leader can set that up by giving some instructions. (A worship leader can also end it quickly if it gets a little off target by simply leading the congregation into the next song!)

4. Pray the Sermon Application.

A pastor often has a key point in the sermon that needs to sink in to the people's hearts. Why not have a time (two to three minutes) where people get into groups of three or four and pray that application into each other's hearts and lives. The pastor needs to give specific instructions so they understand what they are to pray. A bulletin insert or media slide with the important points are all that is needed.

5. Pastor Guided Prayer.

Another excellent way to incorporate prayer is to have the people pray a prayer in unison at the end of the message. The pastor can put a prayer together that reflects exactly the truths and applications he or she wants the people to grasp and live out in their lives. Instruct them to pray out loud after you. Say a phrase and give them time to repeat it. Not only will this do something powerful by praying the application of the message, but people learn to pray. They hear their pastor pray and they begin to understand the kinds of spiritual things they can ask God for in prayer.

6. Have A Time to Pray for Needs.

While this is not corporate prayer in the truest sense, it can be a wonderful time of blessing for your people. Simply put, set aside time in the service where people can pray for others. It can be done a number of ways.

During worship or at the end of a service, have prayer teams (teams of two or three people—a husband/wife team or two males, two females) come forward or line up around the sanctuary. As you sing, people can walk up to a team and be prayed for.

In a smaller congregation it can be meaningful to have people with a need stand where they are. Then have groups gather around them to pray for their need. The congregation keeps worshiping while this is going on.

A note of caution with needs praying: While these are great and meaningful things to do, do not do this type of praying every week if there are no other regular times of visible prayer in your service where you are focused on God's Kingdom agenda. Why? Because you will be perpetuating the false view of prayer that is so prevalent in the Western church: prayer is for me and my needs. Offering loving prayer for people's needs is important, but it should not be the most significant prayer focus in a church that wants to be Kingdom-minded!

SUGGESTION: The book *Praying Grace* (PrayerPoint Press) by Terry Teykl and the DVD set *Upfront* (PrayerShop Publishing) are excellent training resources on this subject of using prayer ministry teams in a service to pray for people. Both are available at prayershop.org.

.: CONCLUSION :.

I consult with a lot of church leadership teams on making prayer foundational to the ministry of their church. Almost every church I work with recognizes that in today's world, it will be almost impossible to start up a weekly prayer meeting if one is not already in place. I always challenge them, if your people won't come to prayer meeting, take prayer meeting to the people. Having times of corporate prayer in the morning worship service can have a profound effect on your people and church. People learn to pray and, through teaching and modeling, develop a heart to pray what is on God's heart.

One of the reasons I suspect that many churches do not experiment with doing some of these dynamic prayer experiences in a service is the "getting away from us" factor. In this era of services being programmed down to the minute and churches having multiple services so they have to get people in and out quickly, prayer that is not fully "controlled" is a dangerous proposition. What happens if someone prays too long or lots of people come up to the microphone to pray?

Most of the suggestions this chapter offers can be easily managed in how much time is allotted. The open microphone is the only one that really might cause a time issue, but even that can be managed if a leader says, "We have time for three or four people," or something like that.

You can also be prepared to cut something else if the prayer time is dynamic and ends up taking longer than expected. If your people who are leading the service understand that you want to offer people meaningful connections to God, and that is happening through this prayer time, then they should hopefully be willing to give up the last song, or—gasp—maybe pastor, you'll have to give up a little of your message time.

And what is the worst that can happen? God shows up, meets His people, and you all spend the service completely overwhelmed by His presence.

CHAPTER 7

..‖ WHAT'S THE PURPOSE ‖.. OF YOUR PRAYER MEETING?

A WHILE AGO, I was engaged as a consultant by a Southern megachurch that wanted to improve as a praying church. In the course of our discussion, the senior pastor shocked me when he said, "I can't recommend our weekly prayer meeting to many believers."

Why?

About eight to ten people attended the meeting (in this church of 6,000). They were sincere people. But they were all seasoned intercessors who did not know what it meant to pray in a public gathering. They all prayed exactly as they would have in their own prayer closet. They practiced personal prayer in a group setting.

Each one who prayed would pray for ten to twenty minutes at a time, covering everything they could think to cover. And some would do so with emotion that was a little "over the top" for those around them. Tears and loud sobbing were a part of it. For the normal individual, it was downright uncomfortable.

This pastor felt—and rightly so—that the prayer meeting would set less mature pray-ers back, rather than teach and encourage them to participate.

.: WHAT'S THE PURPOSE? :.

Asking "What is the purpose of your prayer meeting?" may seem like a silly question. You want to seek God. You want His power, and direction, His will to be released through your prayers. You want to see your church become more dependent on Him. "What do you mean, What's the purpose of our prayer meeting?"

Recently, I participated in leading an evening of prayer at a church. It was the culminating event to a conference that had several speakers. The pastor wanted all of us—him, me, and the other leader—to each feel free to step to the microphone and lead a section of the prayer time. We had a little planning for direction ahead of time, but not a lot.

The prayer meeting was fine as prayer meetings go, but something happened that got me thinking about the purpose of a prayer meeting.

At one point in the service, the microphone was opened to individuals to come up and pray. At first, instruction was given as to some general topics (schools in the area, etc.), but as was typical at prayer meetings, it became a mix of topics that were on the hearts of the pray-ers. What struck me was that the intensity of the praying increased. So much so, that soon the prayer meeting became not participatory for all, but it became a spectator event where the congregation watched as only intense intercessors prayed. After a while we got them back into groups to pray on a selected topic, and the meeting was participatory for everyone again.

When I go into a church and lead a prayer meeting, I have two primary purposes in mind—and neither one has anything to do with seeking God or power, though those are important. I want to show a more dynamic way to conduct a prayer meeting, and I want to do so in a way that will draw in the weakest and most immature pray-er. I do not want to intimidate anyone.

Not all prayer meetings need to have that purpose. Mine do because of what I have been brought in to accomplish in a church when I speak there. I am trying to get the average pew sitter engaged in prayer.

My point is that a good prayer meeting leader should think about purpose when he or she plans the meeting. What do you want to accomplish with this prayer meeting? Do you want it to be accessible to all, or should it be an outlet for the strongest intercessors to go after God's heart? If the former, then you have to watch format and passion. If the latter, then you can't worry that you only have five people coming to the prayer meeting.

If you are calling the meeting in order to "storm the gates of heaven" over a specific situation, then there is no problem with intercessors "cutting loose" and praying strong, bold, emotional, and even long prayers. But if you want to have a prayer gathering that is accessible to every maturity-level believer in your church, then it needs to be formatted in a way where even the weakest pray-er would feel comfortable there and can see how to participate. That probably means restricting the length of individual prayers and having more prayer in smaller groups.

Many churches try to design their primary prayer meeting so it can be a place where any believer can learn, participate, and experience prayer. This means you use a variety of prayer methods, not sticking to the same format week after week. (Remember people's prayer styles?) Make sure that people understand proper protocol when praying in a group: short prayers on one topic, have a leader give the prayer subjects, break up how you pray—sometimes in small groups, sometimes as a large group. If you allow the seasoned intercessors to "cut loose" in this format, soon they will be the only ones praying at these gatherings.

But churches also recognize the need to have a seasoned team of prayer warriors whom it can call on to pray fervently, with no restrictions, over important issues of deep need. Kind of like a prayer swat team! There are times to free those people to pray any way they want. But in most churches, that place is not the weekly prayer meeting that is available to all believers. There might be some times when a subject comes up at a regular all-church prayer gathering where you want these warriors to intercede. That's okay. Let them know ahead of time if you can. But if that is not possible, in the midst of the meeting you could say, "We need our prayer warriors freely to press in on this issue." They will.

Even the Apostle Paul recognized different purposes for prayer and levels of intercession. In Colossians, he told the believers, "Epaphras . . . is always wrestling in prayer for you, that you may stand firm in all the will of God, mature and fully assured" (Colossians 4:12). Here, he referenced an intense level of prayer. But in writing to Timothy, he reminded him that "petitions, prayers, intercession and thanksgiving [should] be made for all people—for kings and all those in authority, that we may live peaceful and quiet lives in all godliness and holiness. This is good, and pleases God our Savior, who wants all people to be saved and to come to a knowledge of the truth" (1 Timothy 2:1-4). All levels of prayer and different types of prayer should be used in praying for the salvation of people. Different types of prayer for different purposes.

SUGGESTION: An excellent resource for a pastor that has much content on church prayer is the textbook, *Giving Ourselves to Prayer* (PrayerShop Publishing), Daniel Crawford, ed. This 584-page, eighty-chapter textbook, designed for seminary students, has twenty chapters on prayer in the church. While not an easy read, it has some great content that can help any pastor or prayer leader navigate this important aspect of prayer in the church. It is available at prayershop.org.

.: WHAT ABOUT MULTI-CHURCH PRAYER? :.

Understanding a prayer meeting's purpose is also important when you try to bring churches in a community together to pray. If you have multiple theological streams of intercessors together, you should still clarify your primary purpose. If it is unity, then you want to do everything you can to assure that it is formatted to appeal to the most conservative church that was invited. Unity is more important than allowing prayer practices that might make some uncomfortable. You want to bring everyone in.

But if your purpose is something else (and it is perfectly fine to have a different purpose)—say to bring intercessors together to do spiritual warfare over your community—then you may not need to worry about making the meeting "comfortable" for every possible participant.

Don't forget to consider these things when you plan your prayer times. Recognize that if the prayer time is geared toward one purpose, then you may not see something you want to see—more people, deeper intercession, etc. Also recognize that your prayer meeting will be more effective if you format it with a purpose in mind. Also remember that if others don't understand or share your purpose, they can work against you. It might be important to explain your purpose with the group so they can understand what you are trying to accomplish and what might be appropriate within that purpose.

.: CONCLUSION :.

Some of you may be sighing, "I just want to get people to come out to a prayer meeting. Now I have to think about purpose, too?" Don't feel stress. It really is not that hard. If you want a gathering accessible to all believers, then a few simple principles need to be put in place.

If it is not important to accommodate the less mature pray-er, that is perfectly okay. But remember that, like my opening illustration, the gathering will eventually reflect the prayer styles of the most dominant intercessors. There is much value in all kinds of prayer and with all kinds of purposes. Lots of spiritual power can come out of that for your church . . . and that is good.

CHAPTER 8

..‖ FROM TWEAKING TO STRATEGY ‖..

WHILE ANY CHURCH can see an improvement in its prayer foundation by simply tweaking existing ministry to include more prayer, the church that wants to see steady improvement will learn that it needs to develop a strategy to grow prayer.

Roughly twenty years ago, Pastor Dee Duke and Jefferson Baptist Church in Jefferson, Oregon, were beginning their journey toward becoming a praying church. God demonstrated His power in an amazing way through a prayer challenge that saw the congregation double in size on Easter and more than fifty people prayed to receive Christ that day. The congregation had been praying specifically for thousands of people by name for months prior to Easter.

That event allowed many to see the power of prayer when it is turned outward. It was a kick start to other prayer ministries and events. But out of it, the church began strategizing and developing prayer ministries that would eventually involve the entire congregation. Today, every member is involved in at least one of its many regular prayer ministries and opportunities. That did not happen by chance.

Like any business that wants to sustain growth, a business plan is a good thing to put together. While the church is not a business, and prayer is certainly not a product to quantify, you will see more results over the long haul if you put together a plan, under the direction of the Holy Spirit of course.

What would you like to accomplish during the next three to five years? What end results do you want to see? Are there any measurable goals you can name? Any behavioral changes you want to see in your people?

.: STARTING POINT TO STRATEGY :.

The first step to developing a strategy is to put a planning team together. You can certainly use your elder board, but in most cases it would be better to have an outside team come together to plan. The team should include the pastor and/or an elder, to both give it clout, to keep it tied to what the leadership desires to see, and to give it a voice with leadership.

At this point, most churches think of the strongest intercessors or those who seem to talk about the importance of prayer all the time as the best candidates for the planning team. You certainly want to include some of those people on your team, but I would not have the entire team made up of them. Why? Because many people who have a significant passion for prayer find it hard to understand why everyone does not. They may find it difficult to relate to the prayer struggler and, as a result, might not plan the best strategies to engage that person.

A better team is one made up of a cross section of your church. All should at least have a heart for prayer and a belief that it is important, but they do not need to be prayer warriors. Have a young mother, an older Sunday school teacher, a high school student, etc.

The best configuration of a team that I ever saw was a team where each of the nine members represented a ministry area in the church. The representative to the team was not usually the leader of that area of ministry either. This model allowed for two important factors: Each member of the team helped the other members grow prayer in their area of ministry; the team had a built-in check to ensure that if an important prayer event was planned that the entire church should participate in, no other events were planned for the same day within individual ministries. Genius!

Once this team forms, the starting point with the team is prayer. Pray about prayer! I would encourage you that the first meeting should be nothing more than perhaps laying out the purpose of the team and then most of the remaining time should be spent in prayer. Ask God for direction, for "a grace of prayer" to fall on your congregation, a renewed hunger for God among your people.

I would also, as much as your budget and resources allow, put together some available resources for team members to read. The best book on growing prayer in the local church is *The Prayer Saturated Church* (NavPress) by Cheryl Sacks. If possible, get a copy for each member or at least enough to pass around. Other resources I recommend:

- "Living in the Upper Room" (PrayerShop) (a small booklet that lays out in a simple way what prayer-based church looks like)
- *Forgotten Power: The Theology of a Praying Church*, the prequel to this book, (PrayerShop Publishing) by David Butts
- *My House Shall Be a House of Prayer* (Pray! Books) Jonathan Graf, editor
- *The Praying Church Handbook* (Alive Publications) by Doug Small.

SUGGESTION: You might want to get several subscriptions to *Prayer Connect* magazine for your team (or a subscription for each member). This publication is loaded with prayer ideas and inspiration to keep one's prayer life fresh.

I would also recommend getting your team connected with the Church Prayer Leaders Network (prayerleader.com) and groups like Harvest Prayer Ministries (harvestprayer.com), Intercessors for America (ifapray.org) and Waymakers (waymakers.org). If your church is a part of a denomination, check with your regional or national offices to see if they have any prayer resources you should be aware of.

Pass the resources around and, at some of the early meetings, discuss what people are reading. What ideas are the resources generating in your team members? Are there some things that seem to resonate with a majority of them?

.: WHERE TO BEGIN YOUR STRATEGY :.

The difficult thing with any strategy sometimes is the first step. Where will you begin? If you are still in the tweaking mode, the obvious starting point would be the area that seems easiest to generate more interest in prayer. Is there an upcoming outreach event for which to generate a prayer base? A ministry launch? Building campaign?

As you develop a long-term strategy, however, it is good to look long range to see first what goals you want to establish. Think about the number of ministries your church has that need prayer input. How many people from your congregation do you desire to see involved in prayer? Think through some targets to hit. This will help you map out what you will do to get there.

There are two parallel streams of strategy you need to plan. First, you need an implementation strategy. What prayer opportunities will you develop and implement? Second, you need a motivation strategy. How will you get people involved? I know a lot of churches that put together an impressive prayer plan (on the implementation side) but fail to consider motivation. They had great ideas of things to do, but failed to get people involved. You need to develop plans for both areas.

.: IMPLEMENTATION STRATEGY :.

When you begin to plan your implementation strategy—what you will do—there are two possible ways to shape your plan.

Most churches need to develop the plan based on their church's mission or vision statement. Take apart the statement and see what areas of ministry fit into it. Then develop your prayer plan keeping in mind that you want to cover the outworking of each area of the statement in prayer. (More on that below.) But for other churches, it might be good to look at what area of outreach ministry seems to be flourishing at the moment, or is there an area of unusual ministry that the Lord has opened up in your church?

For example: I spoke in a Nazarene church in Michigan years ago whose entire prayer ministry started because an unusual number of people in the church developed cancer. Out of love and necessity, the church started praying for those people. As time went on, leaders read as many books on divine healing as they could find (even ones from writers outside their spiritual stream). They went to conferences. And they started seeing healings. Over more time, the church started getting calls from people outside the church asking, "Are you the church that prays for people with cancer? My mother just went into the hospital with breast cancer. Could a team go and pray for her?" And this became an outreach of the church into the community. Out of this prayer, the prayer ministry eventually expanded into other areas.

Another church I know had sixty plus women who started coming to its MOPS (Mothers of Preschoolers) program. Only twelve of the women who came were from the church. Leadership soon realized this was the primary outreach of the church. So they bathed it in prayer. They had families sign up to pray for a woman and her family. They got intercessors to "man" the nursery when MOPS was going on. These ladies prayed for the kids while they watched them and for what was going on in the next room.

You may have a similar situation. Is there a ministry that has an unusual touch into the community? Perhaps you should start developing a prayer strategy there.

But most church prayer teams will choose the mission statement method. Here you begin by dissecting the statement. Most church mission statements have three elements.

Win—Lead people to faith in Jesus Christ

Train—Disciple people into a deeper walk with Christ

Send—Reach people with the love of Christ (missions, local outreach)

As you plan strategy based on a mission statement, you want to make sure there is prayer going on over and within each of those areas.

1. Win—Have you developed tools and a plan to engage

your people to pray for local lost friends and neighbors? What resources do you need to provide? What about motivation to keep praying?

2. Train—What about discipleship? You may want to plan out how prayer is taught in Sunday school classes or small groups. Are the areas of training in your church adequately prayed over?
3. Send—This involves missions. Have you planned how you will engage your congregation to effectively pray for the missionaries your church supports?

Don't let this overwhelm you. Remember, you are becoming a praying church one tweak at a time! As you gather, seek God for His starting point. Pick a few things and plan them well. As they develop, you can move on to other areas.

.: MOTIVATION STRATEGY :.

Besides prayer ministries and events you might plan, you also have to give thought to how to get people to participate. There are four areas you want to consider as you think about motivation.

1. *Pulpit Motivation.* By far the single most significant place of influence is on the platform. When a pastor promotes something to the entire congregation, or when an individual is allowed announcement time for an event, that goes a long way. If you want to become a praying church, a lot needs to be said about prayer and its importance from the platform.

This can become a contentious thing in a church. Why? Many churches have a ban on ministry announcements from the platform. So because the men's ministry is not given platform time to announce its event, the prayer team should not be given time either. Makes sense? No.

Prayer is not another ministry. In Acts, prayer is on equal footing with the Word. The apostles gave themselves to prayer and the teaching of the Word. Just like a church gives lots of platform time to teach the Word, it should give platform time to prayer as well. Prayer makes every ministry more powerful. It is a different thing entirely. That is why the same bans should not apply if you want to be a praying church.

2. *Publicity Motivation.* Advertisers tell us that most people need to see the same message four or five times before they respond. If the only thing you do to promote prayer is put a mention in the monthly newsletter, or a notice one time in the bulletin, you probably will not see a big response. To motivate people to participate in prayer, you need to use every publicity opportunity you can, such as media slide announcements, newsletters, email blasts, posters, skits. Anything and everything.

3. *Opportunity.* Think through the best time to engage people. How can we provide easy opportunity and access to our prayer activities? Do you have mostly families with teens? Maybe a prayer meeting failed to gain traction because it was on the same night of local high school sporting events. Young families? Maybe an event failed because you did not provide child care for young families, so they had to stay home.

These are important things to think about. The church I attended in Colorado Springs saw our monthly corporate prayer meeting die out because we changed venues to save a little money. The free venue was five miles farther from the school we met in, and it was in an unfamiliar church. People stopped coming.

4. *Education.* Something else to think about relates to Chapter 3, "Discipling Your People in Prayer." Many people do not participate in prayer because they do not understand its importance in their life or the life of the church. You may not be able to motivate them to participate until they understand its importance. Something to think about.

.: CONCLUSION :.

Again, do not let this overwhelm you. But if you want to see prayer continue to grow in your church over the long haul, then developing a strategy is very important. Come up with some Spirit-initiated goals and keep talking, thinking, and praying over this important piece to success. But hold on to your plan lightly. Let God guide and direct, but let Him change directions too. A plan is just a guide; it should not be rigid. The Holy Spirit will lead you as you stay open to His voice.

CHAPTER 9

THREE STARTING POINTS TO INCREASE PRAYER

RECENTLY, I DID A STUDY on prayer mobilization in the Bible. I discovered something I thought was interesting: prayer was usually mobilized by a leader challenging the people.

In the Old Testament, we see Nehemiah, Ezra, and Jehoshaphat, to name a few, who challenged people to seek God and provided a venue for them to do so.

Some of you would say, "That isn't the case in the New Testament." The early church was a prayer meeting! Perhaps for the first months and a few years in the life of the early church, people prayed without a lot of encouragement from leaders. But by the time the Epistles were written, we see Paul and James again challenging those under their care to pray.

James's passage in chapter 5 goes through a lengthy encouragement for people to pray more often.

> Is anyone among you in trouble? Let them pray. Is anyone happy? Let them sing songs of praise. Is anyone among you sick? Let them call the elders of the church to pray over them and anoint them with oil in the name of the Lord. And the prayer offered in faith will make the sick person well; the Lord will raise them up. If they have sinned, they will be forgiven. Therefore confess your sins to each other and pray for each other so that you may be healed. The prayer of a righteous person is powerful and effective.

> Elijah was a human being, even as we are. He prayed earnestly that it would not rain, and it did not rain on the land for three and a half years. Again he prayed, and the heavens gave rain, and the earth produced its crops. (James 5:13-18)

Paul asked people to join his missionary endeavors by praying (Romans 15:30; 2 Corinthians 1:11). He also challenged people to "pray without ceasing," to pray when they had anxiety, to pray for those in authority. I suspect all these challenges were made because James and Paul saw the people slacking off in prayer.

Are our people like that?

What's the solution? As leaders—pastors, elders, small group leaders, prayer leaders—we need to challenge people to pray. Your people will not likely pray a lot without encouragement and challenge from you.

In light of that fact, I asked the question, "What prayer opportunities are the most effective in mobilizing a congregation to pray?" In my years of watching churches, here are what I consider to be the three best.

.: ENGAGE YOUR CONGREGATION WITH :. A PRAYER INITIATIVE

A prayer initiative is where everyone prays on a given theme for a set period of time. twenty-four hours, a week, two weeks, a month, or forty days are the most popular. If done well, a prayer initiative is the best way to pull the biggest number of people into prayer. And a number of people will have such a good experience that they will catch the importance of prayer and will be better at it the rest of their lives.

Why is a prayer initiative so effective?

1. Most use Scripture-based prayer guides which both teach people to pray God's Word and move people to pray a Kingdom agenda rather than their own.
2. Because the entire church is involved, people are reminded week after week to participate. There is also a built-in accountability as people hear others talking

about their experiences. That builds within each person a desire to participate even more.

3. Prayer initiatives have a twofold manageable time commitment. First, people are not making a commitment to pray every day for the rest of their lives (while that would be great, it is too scary a commitment for most). Instead, they know they are committing to thirty days or two weeks. But secondly, most prayer initiative guides ask for no more than a one- to five-minute commitment each day. That fact is not intimidating to most people.

Remember, however, a prayer initiative will only work well if it is well planned, prepared for, and promoted. Purchasing some prayer guides a week ahead of the Sunday where you announce, "this is starting today," will not work.

SUGGESTION: Some of the prayer initiatives we recommend are *Seek God for the City, Asleep in the Land of Nod, Revolution on Our Knees,* and *Love to Pray.* While all are good, *Love to Pray* and its forty-days-of-prayer campaign is the one I recommend most often. It has powerful content but also the most developed materials for a church that wants to do a prayer initiative right. Prayershop.org also sells a product called the *Prayer Initiative Sampler Pack.* This packages a single copy of eight different prayer initiatives together at a reduced rate, so you can study them to see which might be the best fit for your church.

For more information, prayerleader.com has some articles on the power of prayer initiatives. (You will find them under Resources-Prayer Leader Central-Extended Prayer Experiences.) Check out:

- "Setting All-Church Prayer in Motion"
- "The Power of a Prayer Initiative"
- "Holding a Week of Prayer"

How good can a prayer initiative be? One stellar example is Mountain View Community Church in Fresno, California. This church of 2,000 holds two all-church prayer initiatives each year, one in the spring and one in the fall. Its pastor, Fred Leonard, explains that because they have new people all the time, he does not want anyone to go very long before they are provided an "on ramp" into prayer.

.: TAKE ADVANTAGE OF A "PASSIONATE" NEED :.

By this I mean three things.

1. **An Unusual Event.** Pay attention when a congregation's heart seems to be focused somewhere. Has something unusual and difficult happened in the life of your congregation—a natural disaster or catastrophe in your community or the world? Is there something going on that naturally moves people to cry out to God? Work hard to rally meaningful prayer events, meetings, groups, times in the worship service, etc., around that prayer need.
2. **An Unusual Common Need.** Pay attention if there is an area of unusual need in your congregation (a lot of people with cancer, a lot of people who lost their jobs due to a local plant's closing, etc.). People's hearts are tender to such things. They can be an opportunity to rally more prayer.
3. **An Area of Unusual Ministry Success.** Is your church experiencing an area of significant ministry? Maybe your youth group is growing all of a sudden,

maybe your Mothers of Preschoolers (MOPS) program has more women in it from the community than from your church. Maybe a significant upcoming outreach event has captured the interest of a lot of your people. Look for those kinds of things and rally prayer around them. God is at work there, which means Satan will be on the attack. This may be an opportunity to get more people praying.

.: HOLD A PRAYER WEEKEND OR CONFERENCE :.

Call the entire church to a special concentrated event to both encourage and challenge them in their prayer lives. This can be very effective to inspire a number of people to go deeper in prayer. And it may not be as expensive as you think.

Many of you have budgets as pastors or prayer leaders and could put on a prayer conference without the leadership of your church suggesting you do it. But for a conference to be truly effective, you need everyone on board. The following factors will make a prayer conference successful:

1. **Supported by leadership.** Pastors and elders will not only promote it, but will model its importance to the congregation by attending. They will also work to see that other events are not scheduled at the same time.

2. **Prayed for.** I notice a difference in a church where I know the event I am speaking at has been well prayed over. Have prayer teams praying even months ahead of the prayer weekend.

3. **Well planned.** Pay attention to the details. Get a planning team together at least four to six months ahead.

4. **Well promoted.** Without proper promotion, it is

difficult for the event to be successful. A few years ago, I was in a church of 600+, where I had given prayer seminars previously, and had even attended the church decades previously when I had lived in the community. Only five people came to my Saturday morning seminars. One lay leader who had known me for years told me the next day that he didn't even know I was speaking that weekend. I noticed there were no posters or announcements of the event anywhere in the church regarding the prayer seminars, even though there were many announcements of other events around.

5. **No competition with other events.** Try to pick a weekend when no other ministry events are planned. Better yet, get it on the calendar and encourage pastoral leadership to put the word out that other events cannot be scheduled for that weekend. The same church that did not promote my event had scheduled two other events that same Saturday morning. The larger the church, the more difficult it is to keep only one event on any given weekend, but you will see more success if it is possible to do.

Here are resources at prayerleader.com that can help you plan your conference:

- "Would Your Church Like to Host a Conference"
- "Plan Your Own Conference"
- Speakers' Bureau

.: CONCLUSION :.

Above all, these events will have far-reaching impact on your church if you promote them. When you hold the event, be it a prayer initiative, special time of prayer, or conference, make sure you promote and highlight the other ongoing prayer opportunities at your church that are available for people to participate in. Put a brochure together that explains various ways each participant can get involved in the regular prayer life of the church. Strike while the fire of their interest is hot!

If you do that, with each of these prayer opportunities, you will see more people catch a passion for prayer and get involved in the prayer life of your church.

CHAPTER 10

DEVELOP PURPOSE IN YOUR CONGREGATIONAL PRAYER LISTS

IN EARLY 2016, I preached at a church in the Midwest. The pastor specifically asked me to teach about Kingdom praying, so I tweaked a message I love to give, entitled "Get into the Battle." This message focuses on the truth that prayer is our primary weapon to grow the Kingdom of Christ.

I arrived a little early for the first service and looked around the church lobby. My attention was drawn toward the church's prayer sheet. It was a 5.25" x 8" card, with one side filled with needs of people. I noticed that the back side of the card was blank. I also noticed there were no ministry prayer requests. Everything on this list was, I assumed, a personal need of people in the church.

An idea came to me as I looked at the card, so I stuck it in my Bible in the spot where I would conclude my message.

TYPICAL DUTY

This church's practice is common in the Western Church. Most churches produce some kind of prayer list made available to those in the congregation who want it. Some smaller congregations put it in the bulletin so all can see what the needs are.

In most cases, the lists are entirely focused—like the Midwest church I visited—on the needs of people. There are lots of health needs, requests for relatives in the military, and a few personal needs other than health—finances, a school issue, car problem, etc. While most requests are about people in the church, often many on the list are needs of people whom most in the church do not know—a second cousin of a church member, a co-worker, or a friend of a friend.

Since I speak regularly in churches, I see lots of these lists. They are very similar. But I rarely see lists that include prayer requests for church-related items, for things that will grow God's Kingdom.

I understand why church prayer lists focus on the personal. One of the ways we show love to others is to pray for their concerns and whatever is on their hearts. I also understand that the "person in charge"—the pastor—often has a pastor's heart. That pastor's heart puts his people's comfort and desires above anything else. So even if pastors wish to teach their people to focus outwardly in their prayer lives, anytime there is a need in the body, it needs to take precedence.

But the challenge comes when outward prayers—prayers for the ministry life of the church—take a backseat to the personal needs.

We do not see this practice when we look at prayer throughout Scripture. When Paul writes to the believers in Colossae, he sends a greeting from Epaphras, who, Paul says, "is always wrestling in prayer for you, that you may stand firm in all the will of God, mature and fully assured" (Col. 4:12). Epaphras was not wrestling over an illness or a new job in someone's life, but over the spiritual health of others.

In Acts 4, following a beating of the apostles and a threat on their lives if they ever preached Christ again, the apostles return to their fellow believers and pray about the situation. Rather than pray the way most of us would in the same situation ("make the situation better, remove the evil men from office, protect us"), they pray, "Now, Lord, consider their threats and enable your servants to speak your word with great boldness. Stretch out your hand to heal and perform signs and wonders through the name of your holy servant Jesus" (Acts 4:29–30). Yes, they expressed, "consider their threats, Lord," but the prayer was primarily to give them the strength and enablement they needed to still proclaim Christ in the midst of the difficulty.

I could be wrong, but I cannot picture the apostles pouring over a modern church list, offering prayers for the everyday stuff that concerns us. Even after they pulled back from the nitty-gritty of ministry to instead give themselves to prayer and the Word (see Acts 6:4), I don't think they let up on their Kingdom-focused prayers.

The answer is not to get rid of church prayer lists. The answer is to make them more balanced between personal and ministry-related needs. Here are a few suggestions to help make this shift in your prayer ministry.

1. Add Relevant Church Ministry Prayer Points.

One of the simplest tweaks is to add specific prayer ministry items to the list. Include a section in the prayer list for prayer points about the preaching ministry, worship, outreach, youth, children's ministry, etc.

If an outreach event is coming up in youth group, get the church praying. If the women's ministry is bringing in a special speaker for a retreat, put that on the prayer list. What about the missionaries your church supports? Why not include recent prayer requests from them?

Include points about the moving of the Spirit in your midst or praying for people to be spiritually hungry. Pray for the pastor's sermon preparation, for ears to hear among the people. Any of those things will help to balance the list.

One of the best prayer lists I've seen was a monthly list used at Shandon Baptist Church in Columbia, SC. (I was there years ago, so I do not know if the church still does this.) The list was an 8.5" x 11" sheet folded in half so it looked like a four-page booklet. There were individuals and needs mentioned in one section of the prayer guide, but half or more of the items on the prayer list were ministry-related. That church understood balance.

2. Remind People to Pray for Kingdom Growth.

Another great way to bring balance is to put prayer prompters along with the needs list, reminding people to pray beyond the obvious. So when you list a believer's need, you might add something like, "Pray that Susan will display the character of Christ to her unsaved loved ones as she goes through this trial. Pray that her family will see the power of Jesus displayed in this situation and will be drawn to Christ."

Think of things you can add as prayer points that will clearly grow the Kingdom of God and bring glory to His Son, Jesus Christ. This will teach your people that God often wants to do things beyond the quick fix in people's lives. It will also help them start thinking about His Kingdom work in your eyes.

Perhaps add a few prayer points that challenge people to pray for a biblical virtue or characteristic for all the believers in your congregation. This point can often come from the current sermon series. Praying a response to the sermon the pastor just preached helps people internalize the biblical principles.

3. Remove Unknown People.
This may sound heartless, but if you want to encourage more people to pray, I would not include in the prayer list a request for someone nobody in the church knows. People grow weary of prayer when they are asked to cover things outside their sphere of knowledge (distant relative, friend of a friend, etc.).

Establishing this policy can also preclude any legal liabilities. Some people your church members know do not want their life situations made known to others. Often those who add people to a prayer list do not think to ask permission to do so. It is not a good practice to allow private information on lists without seeking permission of the people involved.

If you are in a smaller church, there is an exception to this rule. Sometimes a church member has been witnessing to and praying for the salvation of a family member or friend, someone unknown to most. It may be possible to include the name and need of that person on a list seen only in a prayer meeting setting when the witnessing church member is present and can add some knowledge to the request. Then you are probably safe. But I would still not put this person's information on a list available to the entire church.

.: THE IMPORTANCE OF LISTS :.

Prayer lists can still play a vital role in the life of a church. But to make them more effective, I challenge you to more fully develop the Kingdom side of the list to bring balance—and likely more participation from your congregation.

What did I do in the church in the Midwest? As I came to the end of my message and suggested ways to "get into the battle" through prayer, I held up the list. I challenged the congregation to use the list. But I also urged the leadership—in front of their congregation—to fill up the blank side of the prayer guide with church-ministry prayer points!

APPENDIX

SIMPLE IDEAS TO STIMULATE YOUR CHURCH

The following section includes ideas and thoughts that can stimulate you as you consider the direction God wants to take you in developing prayer. These are possible things to think about, try, and maybe tweak so they fit your church. My prayer is that many of them, along with God's leading, your insights, and the knowledge of your church's DNA, will develop into something that can provide encouragement to your people as they grow in prayer.

Let them take you to deeper Holy Spirit-inspired ideas to use in your setting.

They are divided into three categories.

- The first four are discipleship thoughts and ideas.
- The second four are prayer experience ideas you can use in a church service.
- The final seven are general ideas for church prayer.

IDEA 1

A BALANCED PRAYER AGENDA IN A CHURCH

As pastors and prayer leaders, we are all excited when our church increases its prayer practices. Any visible prayer activity in a congregation is good, right? Or is it possible to have unbalanced prayer practices in a church?

While I am for all prayer (provided it is prayer to the one true God through our relationship with Jesus), I do believe it is possible to unknowingly be very unbalanced in the prayer life of a church--even with lots of prayer going on. There are three key areas where a church needs to consider balance in its prayer promotion and practices.

1. Inward versus Outward Prayer

What is the balance between how much time is spent praying for personal needs within your congregation versus time spent praying for Kingdom-advancing items—prayer for lost people, for the moving of God's Spirit in the midst of your congregation, for community transformation, and for the nations (missions, missionaries, completion of the Great Commission, etc.).

In my experience, most congregations focus far more time praying for their own needs than anything else. Some of our practices even foster that. A prayer time in a morning worship service often highlights our own church needs. Smaller churches that may open time up in a service to take requests, will usually only expect to get those types of needs. Even churches that have times where people come forward to be prayed for by teams can be promoting an unbalanced agenda. If that is how visible prayer is always done, it fosters the myth that prayer is to "get my needs fixed."

While there is nothing wrong with praying for people's needs and having practices that provide that opportunity, if that is the only way prayer is used in a congregation, it is unhealthy and unbalanced. Instead, you need to make sure that there are ample prayer opportunities that offer prayer for more Kingdom-advancement requests. Can you have community transformation prayer times from time to time? How regularly do you offer prayer for the missionaries you support, or for nations, or for the people group your church has adopted? How often do you emphasize praying for lost neighbors and co-workers? To have a balanced approach, make sure that people see prayer for more than just their own needs.

2. Seek God's Face Rather Than His Hand Prayer

Similar to the last practice, how balanced is time spent between praying for stuff and just seeking God? Does your congregation regularly see and participate in prayers of praise and thanksgiving from the platform? Do they see prayers from the platform asking for God's presence? Or do they only see prayer that asks for things? If there is not a balance in this area, people's views of prayer and God become skewed. The best place to try to balance this out is through corporate worship.

A good worship leader can use appropriate songs and weave short snippets of prayer that seek God's presence into the worship set or songs that move into times of spontaneous praise or thanksgiving within a worship set. Or a pastor, following a powerful message on worship or spiritual hunger or the greatness of God, can lead his or her congregation into prayers that simply seek God.

3. Personal Prayer versus Praying Together

No one would dispute the fact that in most Western churches, few people pray together. Part of this problem has been fostered by churches that never model healthy corporate prayer. Most church prayer times within a morning worship service amount to one person praying while others listen. While there is certainly a corporate nature to this (and it's a biblical practice—see Solomon at the dedication of the Temple in 2 Chronicles 6-7), it does not help people learn to pray together. They are simply listening in on someone else's prayer.

Instead, people need to be provided with opportunities to pray together . . . and they need to learn how to pray together effectively. They need to be taught not to pray as they would while alone—maybe a long prayer on multiple topics—but to pray shorter prayers that bounce off other prayers, adding to them, fleshing them out, agreeing with them. Churches that teach on how to pray together, and provide opportunities for people to do so, will quickly get this area of prayer in balance.

So you can see that we do need to think about more than just adding additional prayer opportunities for our people. Ask the Holy Spirit to lead you as you consider what might be out of balance in your practices. Taking steps to correct it can bring powerful results to any church.

IDEA 2

..‖ DISCIPLING A CONGREGATION ‖.. THROUGH THE LEVELS OF PRAYER

A number of years ago, I had a pastor friend share how he was concerned that the small prayer meeting at his church was too intimidating so he could not encourage most of his people to attend. The problem was that it was made up of seasoned intercessors who loved to pray. Sounds good, except that the length of the prayers and the emotion with which some prayed was discouraging, or a turnoff, to others.

That is one of the difficulties in moving a congregation forward in prayer. Everyone is at a different level of experience. And while you want to encourage people to go deeper, some of those levels don't mix well. So how do you disciple people at these various levels?

.: THE BEGINNER :.

Probably the biggest lack of training in most churches is at the most simple, basic levels. That beginning believer, that immature Christian who may be a little weak in their faith, how do you get them to see prayer as important, get them to want to learn, and what do you provide for them to grow? This level is overlooked in discipleship for two reasons: 1. It is assumed most new believers will naturally begin to pray—a very false assumption; and 2. Very few materials are available at this most basic level.

A wise prayer leader will work to shore up the opportunities to disciple immature or newer believers. As you plan and strategize, think through these questions:

1. What is the intimidation level of the opportunities for prayer we currently have? Church prayer meeting, small groups, Sunday school classes, corporate opportunities in morning worship service; etc.
2. What type of prayer level does each setting we have cater to?
3. What are the best settings for new believers or immature pray-ers?
4. Can we tweak a setting to make it better for the beginner? Or do we need to start something new?

Once you have analyzed your situation, you are better able to develop a strategy to train and encourage the beginner in prayer.

.: CORE THINGS TO TEACH :.

1. **The Purposes of Prayer.** Why is prayer important? (Relationship with God and the relationship between prayer and releasing God's will on earth.)
2. **Praying God's Purposes.** People need to understand that prayer is not just to get stuff from God to make our lives better. We need to be actively praying for spiritual growth in our lives and the lives of those we love—things like the fruits of the Spirit (Galatians 5:22-23) and the qualities in the Sermon on the Mount (Matthew 5-7), for example.
3. **Praying Scripture.** One of the best things you can teach a new disciple is how to incorporate God's Word into their prayers.
4. **Out Loud versus Silent.** Another great thing to teach a new believer is the benefits of praying out loud (helps you stay on task and prevents your mind from wandering;

has a spiritual warfare dynamic; a shy person who hates praying with others finds it easier if he or she has learned to pray out loud by themselves).

5. **Alone versus Corporate.** People need to learn the importance of praying with other people. There are multiple reasons this is important, but the two most significant things are that it brings unity to the body and it grows the level of faith in a church.

.: AVAILABLE RESOURCES :.

While I mentioned that there were not a great many resources specifically targeted to beginning or immature pray-ers, here are some suggestions for things to use (all are available through prayershop.org).

1. *Love to Pray* by Alvin VanderGriend. This forty-day devotional covers a complete theology of prayer. Each day provides a simple devotional thought based on Scripture, some specific things to focus prayer on, and an action step.
2. *Prayer 101* by Elaine Helms. This book answers some very beginner questions.
3. *The Beginner's Guide to Intercession* by Dutch Sheets. This also provides some simple answers to beginning intercessors.
4. *Patterns for Prayer* by Alvin VanderGriend. This is a 365-day guide that offers a biblical agenda to pray each day for yourself, family and friend, your church, the lost, and the world. It gets people focused on the biblical purposes we should be praying about.
5. *The Power of Personal Prayer* and *Praying Like Paul* by Jonathan Graf. *The Power of Personal Prayer* covers some core topics about prayer, then seeks to take the reader deeper and

deeper into many aspects of prayer. *Praying Like Paul* specifically teaches people to pray for spiritual growth using Scripture.

6. *Solid Foundation* and *Pray the Word* books. These resources teach both the importance of praying Scripture and how to do it.

7. Prayer guides in general. Most people need help thinking of specific items to pray on given topics. Most prayer guides offer Scripture-based prayers or ideas of things to pray. They can be a real boost to beginning pray-ers. Keep a bunch stocked in locations around your church, or better yet, hand some key ones out to everyone.

IDEA 3

..‖ MAKE IT SIMPLE FOR THEM ‖..

For the past twenty years, I have had a burden to see believers discipled in prayer. Most churches neglect this important area probably because they assume prayer growth will just happen in the life of a believer. It typically does not. We need to be intentional about it if we want to see believers grow.

One of the most significant truths I have learned is that good prayer discipleship needs to be simple (more simple than you would think) and basic. Most people are very unsure of themselves when it comes to prayer—either praying alone or with others. These people (many believers in your pews) need the following:

1. **Prayer Guides.** Most guides have Scripture-based prayers that help people learn to pray God's will and heart and get them praying more biblically than simple fix-it prayers.
2. **Motivational Reminders.** Beyond convincing people of prayer's importance, they need encouragement to keep at it. Churches that regularly provide little nudges, visual aides, etc. to remind people to pray, find that more people stick with it . . . and grow as a result.
3. **Nonthreatening Accountability.** In this busy world, it is easy to let things slip. If you want to disciple people effectively in prayer, find ways to add a simple

accountability aspect to your prayer discipleship. Getting people to meet with one or two people for five minutes to pray following a service each week can be a way to provide this accountability.

4. **Meaningful Topics.** People will pray more if they are asked to pray for something that has importance to them. That is why most gravitate to personal needs praying. But you can provide powerful topics that relate to ministry items in your church or community. Give them a good Kingdom agenda to focus prayer on and they will be better at it. Most people need something in their hands that will teach them and help them pray more effectively. That is why books like *Pray the Word for Your Church*, *Prayers That Avail Much*, *Patterns for Prayer*, and *The Common Book of Prayer* are popular. They give people scriptural thoughts on what to pray.

That is also why PrayerShop Publishing and Harvest Prayer Ministries felt it was so important to launch *Prayer Connect* magazine a few years ago. The goal was to give prayer mobilizers—pastors and prayer leaders—a resource that they could put in the hands of average believers to motivate, disciple, and challenge them to pray God's Kingdom purposes.

IDEA 4

..‖ DOES PRAYER JUST HAPPEN? ‖..

Over the years, I've heard a few pithy sayings about prayer. "Prayer is caught, not taught," and "You learn to pray by praying." Both are true, but the effect of these sayings has added to the prayerlessness of many churches. Why? Because they keep churches from being deliberate about discipling in prayer.

These two truths make us assume that prayer will happen naturally. But as I've visited churches across the country, I've observed that it usually doesn't. Without consistent discipling in prayer, the following often happens:

1. **Intimidation.** Newer believers usually hear only mature pray-ers pray in church. Often they think, *I can't pray like that.* As a result, they believe their feeble attempts at prayer are worthless, and they don't pray much.
2. **Hitting the Wall.** New believers and children seem to get more specific prayers answered quickly. Why? I believe God wants to prove Himself to them. Also, they haven't let skepticism enter their prayers. But after a while, most of us reach a place where our petitions don't always bring the same results. Many give up on prayer at this point. But good discipleship would prepare us for this.
3. **Shyness.** Many believers–especially men–are shy about praying in public. Shy pray-ers will not pray with others,

and this can mean death to powerful corporate prayer in churches, in small groups, and in families. Good discipleship in prayer will not let them stay stuck there.

4. **Stunted Kingdom Mind-set.** Believers who don't pray don't grow. The more we pray, the more we are infused with God's heart. And God's heart is for the lost, for the nations. If you want your people to be Kingdom-minded, teach them to pray!

Praying churches are deliberate about discipling in prayer. They make sure that Sunday school classes—at all age levels—regularly provide instruction on prayer. They hold prayer conferences, retreats, and seminars. They train their men in how to pray! And they provide plenty of opportunities to pray, so prayer can be caught and practiced.

Here are some recommendations.

1. **Have organized prayer instruction at least every six months** (every three is better). Teach an elective prayer class in Sunday school, on Sunday night (if you have a meeting then), or in small groups. Look for studies that go beyond simply "prayer as relationship." There are some excellent resources available that take people into Kingdom praying.

2. **Train your leadership.** Many churches are hampered because their elders, deacons, and/or pastoral staff have little sense of expectancy from prayer. Three simple but effective resources to disciple leaders are *My House Shall Be a House of Prayer* (Pray! Books 2002), *Forgotten Power* (PrayerShop Publishing 2015) and "Living in the Upper Room" (PrayerShop Publishing 2013). Another effective tool is *Prayer Connect* magazine.

3. **Focus on teens, young adults, and men.** At the risk of being sexist or age-prejudiced, I believe our most

effective results will come from these groups. First of all, I have observed that women are more naturally drawn to prayer and older believers are more likely to be stronger people of prayer due to life's experiences. Young adults and teens are more driven by experience; they need it and seek it. Since prayer is experiential, our discipleship efforts will more readily take root here. And why men? As linear and pragmatic thinkers, they are more likely to have been thrown by some of the aforementioned problems. And when coupled with God-given authority and headship, a father/husband who prays is a powerful force in the Kingdom!

If we want to see our churches grow in prayer, we must be deliberate about discipling and providing opportunity for people to pray!

IDEA 5

..‖ STIMULATE PRAYER ‖.. THROUGH MULTIMEDIA

Recently I was in Winchester, Virginia, leading a prayer weekend at New Hope Alliance Church. On Sunday morning, the pastor, Ross Halbersma, wanted to turn the Sunday morning service in its entirety into a prayer event—no preaching, just worship and prayer. You can imagine I had no objections to leading that.

As we were talking it through on Friday evening, his wife, Patty, suggested we use Bluetree's song "God of This City" somewhere within the prayer section to stimulate prayer for Winchester. It is a powerful song about God's purposes for a city. Somewhere in our discussion, we decided to include a slide show (Patty is a professional photographer) of rotating photos of Winchester while the song was being sung.

In the service, after it was sung and viewed, the congregation was ready to move into a powerful time of prayer asking God to fulfill His purposes in their city. It was dynamic.

The pastor of my church used that song as well, but in a slightly different way. He and his son had driven around our small town (Brazil, Indiana) shooting video as they went. He preached on evangelism one Sunday, and "God of This City" was introduced to our congregation as the closing song. But our pastor had set up a live microphone at the front of the church. He told people we were going to sing this song and show a video of our community as we sang. "If your heart is stimulated to pray," he said, "come up to the mic and pray. We will still sing while you are praying. So don't worry if we do not hear you. God will." As we sang, so many people came up to pray that we sang the song for fifteen minutes or so.

With current technology and a little ingenuity, powerful times of prayer can be incorporated into a morning worship service stimulated by a media presentation.

Take pictures of congregation members and rotate through them as a stimulus to prayer; have a presentation of photos from your local elementary school, businesses, armed forces, etc. to stimulate focused prayer on those areas. Not creative enough? Why not enlist your church youth group or college and career group to put it together? These groups have kids who understand how to use available technology.

In the Free Download section at harvestprayer.com there are more than 100 PowerPoint slides of prayer quotes. You are free to use them to stimulate prayer in your services.

Go to websites like www.bluefishtv.com and search for prayer. What comes up are a number of excellent short video clips on prayer (some free and some costing $1.99 to $3.99). Many of them can be used as a lead-in to a short prayer time, or simply to stimulate your congregation in the area of prayer.

IDEA 6

..‖ INSTANT PRAYER TEAMS ‖..

Every Sunday, people come to church with burdens. Often it is difficult to even worship with the weights that people carry. Many churches look for effective ways to both recognize that people are hurting and to present those hurts in a powerful way to the Lord. Here is an idea that can do all of this, involve many in your congregation as healing agents and not take a lot away from the flow of the service.

This prayer time is best led by the worship leader, though if everyone is in sync with what will transpire, the senior pastor or an elder or prayer leader can facilitate it. The important thing is to not stop the flow of the service to introduce it. At a point in the musical portion of the worship service, while instruments are playing (preferably during a quieter, slower song), the worship leader (or other leader) has the people sit, and then says something like: "Many are here today with weights and stresses on their lives, perhaps deep hurts. We believe in taking those hurts to God, who wants to heal, restore, transform. We also believe that the body of Christ is to be a family of caring individuals. Today, the body of Christ wants to minister to you who are in need of prayer. In a moment, I am going to ask those who would like prayer to stand. Then we will have believers who are near each standing person (two or three to each person standing) gather around you and pray for God's healing and blessing in your situation. You do not have to share what your need is, unless you want to. People can pray effectively even without knowing details; God knows. Please stay standing if no one sees you right away."

Then the leader asks those who need prayer to stand. As people are standing around the sanctuary, the leader encourages people around those standing to stand and pray for them. The instruments continue playing. The leader and perhaps others are prepared to watch to see if everyone standing gets people around them. If need be, the leader can say, "We need some to pray for a person standing on the left side in the back of the sanctuary."

The first time this is done, you might need to do more preparation—either explain to your church intercessors what they should do, or have elders and other leaders clued in to what will happen, so that they know to get up and pray for others. Be careful that not all those you have alerted ahead of time are leaders. The intent is to get people in the pews to pray for each other.

This can be a meaningful time of ministry that hits a deep need. When I was a worship leader years ago, I recall doing this one Mother's Day. I was led to say that for some, Mother's Day is painful for various reasons. If you are struggling because of what today reminds you of and would like God's peace and comfort, we would like to pray for you. Then I had women stand who wanted prayer. I honestly did not think anyone would want to stand—since it would single them out. But women stood all over the sanctuary. We spent the next ten minutes blessing them with prayers. A number who had been prayed for told me later how much that had blessed them.

IDEA 7

"TRICK" YOUR CONGREGATION INTO PRAYING KOREAN STYLE

Some of us get excited when we are at a prayer gathering where everyone prays out loud all at once. (This is often called Korean-style praying, though truth be told, the church in almost every culture other than Western prays this way.) We would love to see that happen in our churches some Sunday morning, but have little hope. Here is a method that was used by Christ Community Church in Brazil, Indiana, that got everyone praying without fear.

One Sunday morning, ushers handed out "prayer strips" along with bulletins. The prayer strips went to every person who was old enough to read. On each strip was a three-to five-sentence prayer related to some aspect of ministry in the church (though they could be on any subject of importance to you).

At the prayer time, the pastor got up and explained what we were going to do, then he had everyone "pray/read" their prayer, out loud, all at once. He explained that you can expand on the prayer if you want. Everyone participated. The weaker, nervous pray-er simply read his or her prayer out loud. Other more brave souls did that, but they added to it. What resulted was about a minute of a glorious din where everyone was raising their voices to God at the same time.

Besides the Kingdom power of this corporate expression of prayer, there are significant long-term effects. People get used to praying out loud. People begin to see more Kingdom-minded things to pray for other than Aunt Millie's sore foot. Prayer time becomes dynamic.

.: PREPARATION :.

First, you need to come up with three to five Kingdom-focused prayer concerns—preferably about the life of your church. These might be things regarding Spirit-empowered preaching, dynamic Christ-focused worship, transformational power of Christ in your church, and so on.

Second, write out three-to five-sentence prayers for each prayer concern. Use some phrases from scripture, if possible, in each one.

Third, put these on 8.5" x 11" inch paper with space for cutting in between each prayer. Then print them out and cut them into strips of paper, one prayer per strip. You want to have enough strips so every person in the congregation—anyone who is old enough to read—gets one.

Fourth, on the Sunday when you will have this "Korean" prayer time, hand them out to individuals as they come into the sanctuary.

.: FACILITATION :.

Select someone—the pastor, prayer leader, worship leader—to lead this type of prayer. That person will need to be prepared and fully understand what he or she needs to explain to the congregation.

The first time you do this, you will probably need to provide a more detailed explanation of what you are doing. If you are a church with regular visitors, you may need to give the explanation each time. It does not have to be long. Here is a sample of what might need to be said. "As you came in this morning, each of you was given a blue strip (insert whatever color was used) of paper with a prayer on it. Please take them out and look at them. Each prayer is asking God to bless (name your church). In just a moment, I will ask you to pray that prayer—just read it or add to it if you feel led. But we want everyone to read it out loud, all at once. Don't use your shy, timid voice that no one will hear. Use a normal volume—or louder. Don't worry about the person next to you hearing—they'll be praying their prayer out loud, too. When I say go, pray that prayer. Everybody ready? . . . Go!"

It might be a good idea to have instruments play in the background, but that is not necessary. To end the prayer time, as the volume decreases as people finish their prayers—and it will, almost all of a sudden—do one of two things. The leader can pray a short, closing prayer. Or have the worship team take the congregation right into a song.

Easy. When this prayer technique is used, nobody sweats praying out loud, and everyone participates in corporate prayer. It takes a little work ahead of time but can reap "volumes" of prayer rewards!

IDEA 8

..‖ A PRAYER TWIST ON ‖.. A POWERFUL PRACTICE

Most churches have some form of Scripture reading during a morning worship service. It may be in the form of a responsive reading, a recitation by the congregation, or a leader or layperson reading a passage from the platform. The declaration of Scripture is a powerful practice. But with a simple twist from time to time, you can add a dynamic prayer element that can teach your people to pray Scripture.

The idea is not just to recite Scripture or hear it read (there's nothing wrong with that practice, of course), but to add an element where people pray those scriptures into each other or themselves, or their city, neighborhood, and so forth. This can be done in a variety of creative ways with minimal effort.

.: RESPONSIVE PRAYER :.

Instead of having a leader recite a phrase and the congregation read the next phrase in unison as in typical responsive readings, have the leader read a verse or two, then have the congregation recite a prayer, which you provide on the screen or in the bulletin, based on those verses. Go back and forth a few times with three or four sections. This not only allows the congregation to hear God's Word, but it teaches them to pray it.

.: OUTWARD PRAYING :.

After reading a passage relevant to God transforming a community, such as Jeremiah 29:4-7, have the congregation pray prayers related to the content of the passage. You can either provide specific Scripture-based prayers to pray or let them pray their own.

.: PRAYING THE PASTOR'S PASSAGE :.

A dynamic practice that can solidify the points of your pastor's sermon would be to pray Scriptures at the close of the message. Have your pastor tell you what his passage will be, and what applications he wants to leave with people. Then develop some prayers your people can pray that relate to those things.

There are many other creative ways you can add prayer to Scripture reading in a service. The idea is to creatively find ways to show your people how to pray Scripture. If you feel weak in developing Scripture prayer for your congregation, there are prayer guides you can use.

IDEA 9

BECOMING THE ANSWER TO YOUR PRAYERS

Something is happening in Mooresville, Indiana, a beautiful, medium-sized suburb a few miles outside of Indianapolis. Several years ago, pastor Jim Taylor of Grace Missionary Church, while on a sabbatical, was touched by what he was learning about community transformation. Upon coming home, he became a catalyst to bring pastors and churches in Mooresville together to pray for their community.

After a few years, the community started noticing this unity. Its school system came to the pastors' group and asked for help with an issue. One particular school in a section of town was having a huge delinquency problem—way beyond the delinquency rates of its other schools. Would the churches help?

Help they did! They prayed for that school. They rallied their people to volunteer at the school. And they established an after-school care program that included mentoring and tutoring, plus fun things for the kids to do. They got out of their seats and into the streets! The result? The next year, that school had no serious delinquency problems!

That story is starting to multiply itself over and over in cities around the country—and the world. The Global Day of Prayer's challenge to do acts of kindness for ninety days following the day of prayer is seeing churches do tremendous things in their communities. In Dallas, churches are cleaning up neighborhoods and parks and repairing houses. As a result, their opportunities to share the gospel are multiplying. The fact is churches that are coupling prayer with community involvement are seeing

God open amazing doors in their cities.

In Jeremiah 29, Jeremiah challenges the people who are in exile in Babylon to "get out of their seats and into the streets." If ever there was a time to hunker down and stay out of sight of the outside world, it would be that situation. But he says, "Seek the peace and prosperity of the city to which I have carried you into exile" (verse 7). He tells them to build and buy homes, have their sons and daughters marry there, do commerce. In other words, live life in a way that benefits their community. Don't stay in a little enclave.

If you want to see your church do more to influence your community, start praying for community transformation. Then don't be surprised if God starts to move your people to "get out of their seats and into the streets." And don't worry if you don't have any specific things on your mind to do in your community. Start with prayer and God will reveal exactly what He wants your church to do! Jeremiah goes on in chapter 29 to talk of God's plan to prosper His people. But he says, you will find God's plans as you "call upon [Him] and come and pray to [Him]. . . . You will seek [Him] and find [Him] when you seek [Him] with all your heart" (Jer. 29: 12-13).

IDEA 10

TWEAKING OUR REQUESTS

A century ago, Bethany Street Presbyterian Church in Philadelphia had an unusual season of people coming to faith in Jesus Christ—more than 1,100 in a three-year period. Possibly more remarkable was that more than 600 of those converts were men. Bethany's pastor, Rev. Wilbur Chapman, attributed this outpouring to a group of 200 men who were meeting to pray before services every Sunday morning.

These men were not praying for the needs of Bethany. No bad back was mentioned, no swollen knee, not even a new job for an out-of-work member was lifted up. This group was focused on one thing: that the Holy Spirit's power would fall on their pastor as he stepped into the pulpit to preach!

I believe this church was thriving in its Kingdom work because of the emphasis of those prayers. They were not the "make everyone's life good" prayers that so often seem to be the focus of most church prayer.

Today's churches and prayer leaders are coming up with better and more creative ways to focus prayer on the needs of their churches. Email prayer bulletins are replacing prayer chains. Creative bulletin inserts are printed so those who can't make it to the prayer meeting can still pray. But even with these new delivery methods, it is still too easy to fill them with the "fix-it" prayer needs of a congregation, rather than the spiritual life and health needs of the Kingdom work of the church.

We need to strike a balance between space and time given to praying for personal needs and the space and time given to Kingdom issues. And we need to take seriously the chance to disciple a congregation in prayer through the requests we give them.

It is very easy to put someone in charge of collecting requests for an e-prayer list. They can effectively function like clockwork—pull the request in, type them up, send them out—every month. No sweat. Our needs are being prayed for each month. But if you want your people to grow in their effectiveness as Kingdom intercessors, you need to take the content of those prayer lists more seriously. Church prayer lists can be Kingdom driven. They can move your people to pray for spiritual issues in your church. We just need to take the time to tweak those lists.

One simple step would be to make sure there are more requests for ministry issues than for personal needs on the list. Calvary Chapel Port St. Lucie (Florida) has two of the three pages on its weekly prayer sheets focus on ministry issues. You think when their people see that two-thirds of what they are asked to pray for are ministry issues this won't change the way they pray? Not only does this bless the church spiritually, but it disciples people away from a "prayer fixes things" mentality.

I believe what happened in Bethany Street Presbyterian Church a century ago can happen in churches today. Who knows? Simply altering the focus of our people's prayers may put us in a position to receive this kind of a blessing.

IDEA 11

..|| HOLDING A WEEK OF PRAYER ||..

A week of prayer. The thought of that scares most pastors and prayer leaders. They think, *I can't even get people to come to one prayer meeting; how am I going to get them out to a week of prayer meetings?*

But if done correctly, with good promotion both from the pulpit and everywhere around the church, you would be surprised at what transpires.

There are lots of ways to hold a week of prayer, but the best ones actually bring people together a number of times (every night?) for prayer experiences. Many churches set up a room with prayer stations for 24/7 prayer, or for prayer from 6:00 a.m. to 10:00 p.m. People can come and go throughout the day or night.

Here are some thoughts on how to make a week of prayer effective. Is everyone on board? For such a week to succeed, leadership in a church—pastor, board, elders, deacons, whoever "is in charge"—needs to feel a week of prayer is important. For a week to be successful, it is important that pastors, staff, and leaders attend as many evenings as possible. While a pastor does not have to lead every prayer meeting during the year, your pastoral staff and elders should lead each evening of a week of prayer as a statement to the church.

Shut everything down. For a week of prayer to succeed, it is also important not to allow any ministry to function that week (unless absolutely necessary). No small groups, no Bible studies, possibly even no other prayer groups should hold regular meetings. Instead, each person should be encouraged to come to as many evenings of the week of prayer as possible.

Be creative. If this is to become a major event in the life of your church, much effort should be put into it. Look for ways to shake people up from their typical prayer practices. No two evenings should be the same. No evening should be the same as the prayer meeting you do every week. Resources such as *And the Place Was Shaken* (John Franklin), *Fresh Encounters* (Daniel Henderson), and *A Year of Prayer Events for Your Church* (Sandra Higley) can provide helpful ideas. (All are available through prayershop.org.)

Give lots of help. People who do not pray a lot, and who are not used to praying together, will be nervous. You need to give them guides, Scriptures, and prayer points to pray. This will ease their fear and give them a good experience (which will draw them next time).

Promote well. Since this could well be the most important event in the church calendar, you need to promote it that way. Start promoting at least a month or two ahead. Plaster your church gathering areas with posters. Bulletin announcements each week, a newsletter article, post it on your website, and plenty of talk from the pulpit are also key. A few years ago, I spoke at Rexdale Alliance Church in Toronto, Ontario, Canada, as the kickoff to its annual week of prayer. In each service, it had a young woman (early thirties) share a testimony about what the week of prayer did in her life the previous year. It was a powerful draw. In a Saturday night worship and one Sunday morning worship, Pastor Krishnan had people come to a mic and pray, asking God for what they wanted Him to do in them during the week. At the Saturday night service, this went on for forty-five minutes as a powerful "presence of God" moment took place. Your people need to see that this is not an option to them, but it is important to the life of their church—and their spiritual health as well.

If you start to put such a prayer week into your calendar, it becomes known that you value this enough to hold one each year. Put effort into making it meaningful for all, and you will see it build and prayer rise a notch in the life of your church.

IDEA 12

OUR DEVICES OR GOD'S AGENDA?

I was recently in a church in a denomination that was voting on merging with a second denomination. The Sunday I was there was the last day members could vote. I overheard the member in charge of the voting trying to collect a vote from another member. The member who hadn't yet voted wanted to pass because she didn't know what it was all about. But the vote collector tried to push her to vote.

I thought to myself, *She obviously hasn't prayed about the situation, and is wisely abstaining.* We would all agree: Making significant decisions without much prayer is indeed foolish.

But how many decisions do we, as individuals and churches, make without getting a clear answer from the Holy Spirit? Probably quite a few. Oh, we all pray at the beginning of a board or elders' meeting, or before a vote at a congregational meeting, but does that always give us clear direction from God? I, for one, do not think so.

Jesus sought direction from the Father, often by praying all night. If you look at every time Scripture says that Jesus went away (night, early morning, etc.) to pray, you will find something interesting. Each time Jesus did that, immediately afterward he either made an important decision or changed direction in His ministry.

Luke 6:12-16 shows us that He prayed all night before selecting theTwelve. Mark 1:35-39 reveals a time Jesus prayed and Peter interrupted Him because there were so many people looking to be ministered to. Yet, Jesus said, "Let us go somewhere else—to the nearby villages—so I can preach there also." He changed direction despite obvious ministry needs before Him. Clearly, Jesus used those deep prayer times to get His marching orders.

How much more do we need those times of prayer—both individually and especially as churches. But they are certainly rare these days. Thinking that we can do it, Westerners that we are, it's not easy being dependent on God for direction. We have everything we need to make logical decisions—and we do. That, plus being used to "instant everything," does not make for the patience necessary for the "God, we need to understand your heart on this," decision-making process.

I wonder if that isn't the reason so many of our churches are stagnant, status quo churches that have not seen growth—numerically or spiritually—in years. We have left seeking God out of the mix in how we operate. When we fail to seek God's agenda, we depend solely on the latest church growth or leadership books; we are at the mercy of the controlling board member who always gets a convenient "check in his spirit." We can only go as far as our human resources will take us (certainly not into God's immeasurably more than all we could ask or imagine!—Ephesians 3:20).

What would happen if we all went back to the truth of Jeremiah 29:11-13 (which are corporate verses, by the way, written for a group). If we will seek God with all (meaning collective) our hearts, we are going to find the plans He has for us. And Jeremiah says they are plans to prosper us, plans to give us a hope and a future.

How about a new pattern? Pray for forty-five minutes to an hour before board or elder meetings. Have half- or all-nights of prayer as important decisions loom (or even just to show your dependence on God!). Develop a weekly, biweekly, or monthly prayer meeting solely with the purpose of seeking God for direction (no needs-praying). And if the people won't come to you, bring prayer to the people. Turn some Sunday morning services into prayer meetings if need be.

We are desperate for spiritual power once again to come into our churches. Seeking after God's agenda, rather than relying on our own, is a huge step in that direction.

IDEA 13

BEST WAY TO CHANGE A PRAYER MEETING FOR THE BETTER

There are lots of issues involved when a church is bogged down in a prayer meeting rut. And there is no simple fix to make an existing, dull prayer meeting exciting. But in almost every situation, there is one change you can make that will vastly improve the prayer.

What is it? Take the ownership of what you pray for away from the people and give it to a leader. In other words, let a leader select the prayer focus. This makes it easier to focus the meeting on Christ and not on the attendees. Most prayer meetings are people led, and focus on the agenda of those who attend. It is difficult to grow these prayer meetings to more than a few people. Why? Because when it focuses on the people's agendas, it functions like a small group. People who are not on the "in," who don't know who or what is being prayed for, will have no interest in be a part of the meeting.

However, if a leader can change the focus so the prayer agenda are items of interest to a broader group—Kingdom things regarding the church, community, nation—there is a better chance to grow the group and to be more dynamic. An outward focus makes for more passionate prayer than the typical inward focus of individual needs.

While an existing group may fight a change, it is well worth a try. Start out gently. Don't change the whole prayer meeting, just start with fifteen minutes of it. Explain that you want to begin with everyone praying for ten to fifteen minutes on one topic—then give the topic. Explain that after that, you can all pray the way you have in the past.

Not everyone will like it, but hopefully enough in the group will recognize that the prayer time at the beginning was more engaging and will become supporters of doing it again.

IDEA 14

IS WARFARE NEEDED?

It was an odd thing. As I preached that Sunday morning, every time I stepped into the area immediately behind the pulpit, I struggled to collect my thoughts. When I wandered to either side, my mind was clear and I could speak with ease. I thought my mind was playing tricks on me or that I was giving into suggestion. You see, the pastor told me how difficult it was for him to preach from behind the pulpit. Now I was experiencing this phenomenon myself.

Today, in the United States, there is almost no positive church growth occurring anywhere. Most churches that are growing are doing so by pulling sheep from other less-exciting churches in their communities—not by people coming to Christ. Most denominational church leaders will tell you their churches are full of infighting and lack of commitment. Many—if not most—churches are either status quo or in decline.

With this reality, why do we not think to look for spiritual strongholds or bondages in churches as a possible cause? Very few churches—including charismatic/Pentecostal churches—are thinking of the issue of church cleansing. Yet tens of thousands of churches have suffered serious "Satan's won a victory" situations in their past. Church splits or new church starts led by a disgruntled person who left a former church staff, sexual misconduct of clergy and leaders, power control issues of leading families who want to run things are all circumstances that give Satan strong footholds into a church. And in our "avoid conflict" way of operating, we want to simply overlook these.

Many of us struggle to see things through spiritual eyes. I have a pastor friend who was faced with a situation where a person on his worship team was obviously struggling with some demonic things in his life, yet the pastor was very apathetic to do anything. Get him into counseling (something he had been in for years) was his approach. The thought of bringing in someone to teach leaders on spiritual warfare was distasteful to this pastor. He looked back to one experience in seminary where he had watched a deliverance session prove fruitless. Sadly, that one experience had constructed a wall to this spiritual dimension in him.

Pastors and prayer leaders, it is time to open our eyes. Virtually every church that has been around for any length of time has the potential for serious spiritual bondage issues. Satan wants to make the church ineffective—and he has succeeded in many places. If your church is stagnant, it is time to seek God for the cause.

If this is new to you, I highly recommend getting help. Some basic resources on the topic are *The Devil Goes to Church* (prayershop.org), *The Believer's Guide to Spiritual Warfare* by Tom White, and *Bondage Breakers* by Neil Anderson. Look for people and ministries who can help you.

When Jesus was challenging Peter about his leadership in the soon-to-be-formed church, He said, "On this rock I will build my church, and the gates of [hell] will not overcome it" (Matthew 16:18-19). Many of us miss something unique in this verse. Jesus talks about the gates of hell. We often think of spiritual warfare as defensive. But this verse is talking about taking the offensive where Satan and hell are concerned. You see, the gates of a city do not move. They are not an offensive weapon; they are a defensive measure. We are to attack the gates of hell. If we would go on the offensive and attack our church bondages and strongholds, we would see a vastly different church. A victorious church!

Where do we begin? Pray! Seek God for direction. Ask Him to reveal if there are issues that have never been dealt with in the life of your church.

IDEA 15

..‖ A SIMPLE REMINDER TO PRAY ‖..

If you are like me, I forget to do things. I have to make a list when I go to the store or I will forget a crucial item. I need to use the event reminder on my phone or computer or I will miss an important conference call. And "to do" lists of chores are important to me as well. Because I need to be reminded, I got the idea a number of years ago that maybe reminders for prayer would be a good idea as well.

So I went to work to try to imbed in my mind that I should pray about a specific thing every time I see some common item. For example, I made a particular traffic light I went by regularly a reminder to pray for my pastor. I reminded myself to pray for my daughter every time I saw her bedroom door.

Reminders are a great way to stimulate prayer on certain issues. Believers of all ages can be taught to pray when they see something. Kids are taught to pray for whoever is hurting when they hear a siren or see an ambulance or fire truck go by. That's why missionaries hand out cards with their picture on them. "Stick this on your refrigerator so you are reminded to pray for us." Churches have used crosses with names of the lost on them, pictures of lighthouses, etc., to stimulate prayer for lost people.

The next time your church wants to rally prayer around an issue or topic, consider using some symbol people would see regularly as a reminder to stimulate prayer. Tell people "when you see ________, pray for ________________."

One of the best reminders I ever saw was used by the men of a church in the Seattle area. I was speaking on prayer at their men's retreat.

As a wrap-up, the senior pastor gave each guy (more than sixty of them) a restaurant-sized bottle of Tabasco sauce—"hot sauce." He told them to put it where they would see it every day. (He recommended their shower.) Then he said, "Tell your wife why it's there so she won't throw it away." Finally, he said, "When you see it, I want you to pray for two things: pray that I'll be red hot for God, and pray that you'll be red hot for God." What a great way to get the men of his church praying one of the most powerful prayers they could pray!

Think about reminders the next time you rally people to pray for a period of time.

..‖ FINAL THOUGHTS ‖..

So that's how you become a praying church one tweak at a time.

Discern what areas of prayer God wants you to focus on, and what ideas seem the best fit for your church. Begin to implement them and you will start to see prayer become more and more the norm in your church. As that happens, you will see real spiritual change.

You will begin to see the power or the Holy Spirit restored in your midst.

Jonathan Graf is available to help your church grow in prayer. Through Harvest Prayer Ministries, Jon offers consulting and teaching services that can be targeted toward what your leaders and congregation need to make prayer more foundational in the life of your fellowship.

Through a plan called "Roadmap," Jon can guide your leadership team into discerning God's will and mapping out the direction you need to take on your journey toward becoming a praying church.

Contact him at (812) 238-5504 or jong@harvestprayer.com.

Harvest Prayer Ministries
P.O. Box 10667
Terre Haute, IN 47801

(812) 238-5504

www.harvestprayer.com

www.ingramcontent.com/pod-product-compliance
Lightning Source LLC
LaVergne TN
LVHW020754241026
850861LV00033B/390
9781935012665